LEARNING TO LIVE FROM THE

PARABLES

TIMELESS STORIES
JESUS TOLD ABOUT LIFE

MORRIS M. WOMACK

COLLEGE PRESS
PUBLISHING COMPANY
Joplin, Missou

D1056859

Library of Congress Cataloging-in-Publication Data

Womack, Morris M.
    Learning to live from the parables: timeless stories Jesus
told about life / Morris Womack
        p.   cm.
    ISBN 0-89900-728-7
    1. Jesus Christ—Parables. 2. Christian life—Churches of
Christ authors. I. Title.
BT375.2.W66 1995
226.8'06—dc20   95-6359
                                                        CIP

TABLE OF CONTENTS

PREFACE

This book on the parables is the fulfillment of one of my life's dreams. In 1946, I heard C.E. McGaughey deliver a series of lessons at the Freed-Hardeman College annual Bible lectures on the subject of the parables of Jesus. I was so impressed with these lessons that I made a promise to myself that someday, if the Lord was willing, I would write a book on the parables of Jesus. I had been introduced to the parables in a young people's class at the Central Church of Christ in McMinnville, Tennessee. Bro. M. Kurfees Pullias had taught those classes, and I fell in love with the parables.

Ever since those two introductions to the parables, I have cherished them with an indescribable joy. They have been a source of inspiration to me through the years. I have gathered a sizable collection of books on these stories of Jesus, have preached on them many times, and have taught them in Bible class situations more times than I can count.

My goal for this book has changed during the years. At first, I had thought I wanted to write a book focused on the more technical aspects of the parables. As I have matured, I have drastically changed my intentions. I have come to believe that these lessons from the teachings of Jesus give us much help in focusing our lives on Christ. My intentions changed, and this book is now focused on helping all Christians, hopefully on all levels of educational and Christian maturity.

So often, when people want to read uplifting and encouraging Scriptures, we frequently refer them to the Psalms. There is no question that the Psalms are a storehouse of encouragement and spiritual guidance. But, I believe that the Parables of Jesus can also become a source for us to use to learn to live our lives more completely; hence, the title "Learning to Live From The Parables." I hope that as you read this book you will find it helpful and encouraging as you face your daily problems and challenges. The parables are literally as close to the teachings of Jesus as you can get. We need to return to more study of the life and teachings of Jesus.

No book is ever the product of any one person. I am especially indebted to many people for helping me make this dream come true. Many of my former fellow-students have encouraged, and often doubted, me in accomplishing this goal. Thanks to each one of them. Nearly a half century has passed since I first determined to begin this task. Many Christians in many congregations have encouraged me, made suggestions, given me insights, and in so many other ways have assisted my efforts.

But on a more personal and intimate level, I owe an unbelievable word of thanks to my wife, Ada, to my children Jim (now deceased), Dick, and Leanne, who have always believed in me even in my darkest hours. They have encouraged me when I was almost as low as I could get; they have helped to humble me when I may have been too proud. But, they have been there! They have tired as I rehearsed over and over my dreams and understandings of the parables. Thank you, my dear family.

One of the most valuable helpers in this project has been Bill Henegar, assistant vice president of Pepperdine University. Bill consented several months ago to critically read this book. He has done an invaluable service in helping me correct typographic errors, reword and edit many phrases, and in making many suggestions to help us understand these parables. Bill, thank you for not only being a friend and a loyal brother in Christ, but also for being a great helper in this project. Then, I could not forget John Hunter and Steve Jennings of College Press. These gentlemen have been so helpful in advising me and in having faith in me as I wrote.

To you, and everyone, who will take time to read these words and the chapters to follow, it is you that I owe an especially great debt to. You honor me by reading and hopefully becoming stronger by having read. May God bless you as you read and as you live the good life of faith for Jesus Christ, for whom all things have been done.

This book is lovingly dedicated
to

Ada (my wife), Dick (my son) and Leanne (my daughter)
for their loyal support, encouragement, and patience
in all that I have attempted to do;

and to

Bill Henegar, my friend, my brother, and my encourager,
for all the many hours he spent in helping me
prepare this book for publication.

INTRODUCTION: LEARNING THE ESSENCE OF LIFE

They called Him "Teacher," (John 3:2) and a teacher He was. But, the fact is: He was infinitely more than that. He was the Master Teacher! He was the Teacher of teachers. When the temple guards returned to those who had ordered Jesus' arrest, they reported, "No one ever spoke the way this man does" (John 7:46).

What was it that made this "Teacher of teachers" so special? In this chapter and the ones to follow, we will see why Jesus is truly the Master Teacher.

Jesus, the Master Teacher

The Criteria of a Good Teacher. A good teacher is many things: an instructor, a model, a counselor, a mentor. Jesus was all of these to His disciples; and He is all of these to each of us. Jesus possessed the attributes which are essential for the teacher. Four criteria of a great teacher exhibited by Jesus will be noted briefly. First, *He possessed superior knowledge.* Good teachers must have great knowledge. Jesus knew the Father (John 14:5–11), and He declared the Father to the world. He had a superior knowledge of His audience (cf. Rev. 2:2). He could even know the thoughts and needs of people before they asked Him. Second, *Jesus had a superior message.* His message was about the Kingdom of God and how salvation is provided for those who are citizens of the kingdom. Third, *Jesus was known by his fruits.* How sad for a teacher to have many wonderful attributes but to be barren as a teacher because the fruits of his teaching are lacking. One who does not *live* his/her teaching becomes an anathema to the very message that has been taught. Fourth, *Jesus had superior teaching methods.* One may have great knowledge and a powerful message, but unless one also has appropriate teaching methods, the message may be lost. Jesus used a number of methods: the lecture method (e.g., the Sermon on the Mount, Matt. 5, 6, and 7); question and answer (Matt. 22:41–45); life situations (the Samaritan, John 4:2–26); rhetorical questions (Matt. 22:18–21); and parables. This series of studies will focus on the lessons we can gain from just one of Jesus' teaching methods: His storytelling through the use of parables. Jesus is the prince of "parabolia."

As a teacher, Jesus has never had an equal. Some of the other characteristics of Jesus as a teacher are worth noting. For example, He was natural and informal, not pompous nor proud. He spoke *to* the people, not *at* them. He also was a teacher of the people, not a logician or a systematic teacher. This does not mean that He was illogical or unsystematic; rather, He was more interested in teaching people on a common plane. His message was often picturesque, not always literal and boring. He used lessons from life and human experience. In addition, His message was clear and easy to understand, not hidden except from those not wanting to learn.

The Message of Jesus. Never in the history of humanity has a more profound, more incisive, more influential message been given. Jesus' message has conquered the hearts of a large segment of the world's population; it has also influenced other messages that have not, in fact, subscribed to His ultimate authority and Lordship.

The "kingdom of God" was central in Jesus' message. The

Jewish nation had been looking for the coming of the kingdom of God for centuries. Finally, at long last, John the Baptist heralded the nearness of the kingdom (Matt. 3:1–2), and he also announced the imminent arrival of the King. Not long after, when Jesus began His personal ministry, the kingdom of God was central in His message. In fact, the kingdom message is one of the central messages of the parables of Jesus. This will be discussed in more detail in a later part of our study.

A careful study will reveal that the essence of Jesus' teaching is found in the parables. He stated that He came to bring "life" to humanity (John 10:10). In fact, He heralded the coming of *"abundant"* living, or life "to the full."[1] In the parables, Jesus looks at abundant life in its day-to-day setting — situations and relationships which we regularly face are discussed. In the parables, we learn how to put life together in its proper perspective.

The heart of this entire study is the message of Jesus, and one of its major purposes is "Learning to Live" from the parables. More will be said about this later. All too often, we have learned and taught the message of Christ as though it were limited to the Epistles. All of the New Testament is inspired of God, and yet I submit to you that God's central message to us is found in the four accounts of the Gospel of Jesus Christ. *This* is the primary place we need to go to learn what Jesus teaches us.

If we are to "learn to live" from the parables, we must understand the *meaning* of Jesus' message. The parables were the central element in the methodology of the Master Teacher. As such, they surely express the central message of Jesus.

The social, political, and religious climate in which Jesus began to revolutionize the thinking of the world was certainly different from that of our day. Obviously, this does not mean that His message is not applicable to us today; but it does mean that we should understand the cultural climate of that era and be able to apply His message within the social, political, and religious climate of our own time.

What was the message of Jesus? It would be a gross error to assume that an exhaustive explanation of the totality of Jesus' message could be given in a few paragraphs. But, at the risk of appearing simplistic, I suggest that the heart of Jesus' message can be summarized in four persistent themes which Jesus stressed: *Sin* (its guilt and forgiveness), *Submission* (kingdom living), *Servanthood* (counting others better than self), and *Salvation* (both here and hereafter).

Jesus taught that *Sin* is ever-present among mortals, for we are all sinners. He never approved of sin, yet He was loving and sympathetic to the sinner. In His teaching, we learn of the nature, curse, and cure for sin and this is impressed in His parable teaching. *Submission* is necessary for us to be acceptable to God. Jesus taught and illustrated the meaning and nature of obedience, or submission. And it is through obedience that we learn the true meaning of service. *Servanthood* is a central focus in Jesus' teaching. He indicated that the road to greatness is on your knees. Life takes on true meaning only as we learn humility through obedience and as we count others better than self. Finally, Jesus revealed that *Salvation* begins in this life. We are initially saved from ourselves, from our own selfishness, in order that we may look to Jesus, the giver of the greatest reward that life can claim. We not only have life (salvation) in this life, but ultimately life in the world to come.

The problems facing the church and individual Christians today are many; but the one central problem facing them is a lack of focus on Jesus. Christ must become *central* in the life of the church and in the life of each Christian. This is the focus of His message: we must position Him in the most central place in our lives. Jesus has experienced life at its best and at its worst. By placing Him at the heart and helm of our lives, He can direct us as we strive to please Him.

Life is a constant learning experience. We often think that life would be great if it were not for the problems we face. But it is through those problems that life becomes meaningful. Living is always "becoming," but never completely arriving. Our lives are continually changing, and we must learn to adapt to those changes.

Understanding the Parables

Learning to Live from the Parables. Many books have been written about the parables of Jesus. Every writer has some specific reason for writing about them. This study has one central focus: "Learning to Live" from the Parables. It is a study, therefore, about life! Jesus' purpose in coming to earth was to bring life. "I have come that they may have life, and have it to the full," He said (John 10:10).

If the parables concentrate on "Learning to Live," as I believe they do, they need to be studied as *living* messages. One characteristic of the parables that needs to be constantly impressed on our minds is the fact that they are all life-situations. They were either true, or they were capable of being true. Unlike the fable, common in Jesus' day, the parables were lifelike. In fact, it is highly possible that some of the parables that Jesus told were *actually* true incidents. Therefore, two principles will be followed in our study: (1) The parables must first be seen in their original context; and, (2) They must then be applied to modern living. The parables are never outdated. They have to do with real life.

The Scriptures have always been a great source of personal and spiritual comfort. We often see suggested readings for those who are having various emotional and spiritual needs, and often these come from the Psalms. In this study, we want to redirect our thinking, because the parables of Jesus are also a source of comfort. Although the Psalms of David and others are a storehouse for spiritual strength, you are challenged to look to the words of the Lord Jesus Christ with the same perspective. In the "Learning to Live" section of each lesson, diligent effort will be given to point out how the various parables may serve as your source of strength. Perhaps the parables will provide a mirror of ourselves as we look inwardly throughout this study.

The Importance of the Parables. As stated earlier, the parables are the heart of Jesus' teaching. Dr. Neil R. Lightfoot wrote:

> The parables comprise more than one-third of the recorded teachings of Jesus. The Master of all teachers often puts men to thinking by using pictures. He did not leave principles in the way of life in abstraction, but brought them down within reach of the "humble doers."[2]

So important was the parable in Jesus' teaching experiences that it was said on one occasion that He did not "say anything" without using a parable (Matt. 13:34). Obviously, Jesus did not limit His teaching to the parabolic method only but a large portion of it is in parables. All of the parables that we will study are found in the Synoptic Gospels (Matthew, Mark, and Luke). It is interesting to note that none of His typical parables are found in the Gospel of John.

What Is A Parable? Before we define the parable, it might be helpful to compare it with some other types of illustration. The *fable* is a well-known communication tool. We are all aware of Aesop and his famous fables, as well as others. The fable differs greatly from the parable. In a fable, non-human and inanimate things are often given human traits. A popular fable is the race between the Tortoise and the Hare. However, there is a fable in the book of Judges (9:7–15) told by Jotham, concerning the trees trying to anoint for themselves a king. William Smith observes that "As a form of teaching, the Parable . . . differs from the Fable, (1) in excluding brute or inanimate creatures passing out of the laws of their nature, and speaking or acting like men, (2) in its higher ethical significance."[3]

The parable also differs from the analogy. In the analogy, each item of the figure of speech has a counterpart for which it stands. Now, it is true that some of Jesus' parables (for example, the Parable of the Tares) resemble an analogy. But, this is the exception, not the rule; and even when this occurs, it is not a true analogy.

At one time, many thought that Jesus created the parable. However, there is ample evidence to show that Jesus did not create the parable; parables were used long before Jesus' day, both in theological as well as secular situations. We now have a number of instances of parables from biblical as well as non-biblical sources. In the Old Testament, the term translated "parable" is משל (mashal). It literally means "a similitude or comparison." It is also used to refer to a "proverb." One of the best-known parables in the Old Testament was given by Nathan to David concerning David's adulterous act with Bathsheba (see 2 Sam. 12:1–14). There are other parables related in the Old Testament, especially in Ezekiel.

"Parable" in the New Testament is a translation of the Greek word παραβολή (parabole), which is actually a combination of two words. It literally means "a throwing alongside of." Often, a parable is defined as "an earthly story with a heavenly meaning." This is a good definition, but it does not go quite far enough. A parable is a realistic story in which we see ourselves in it, but not until we are "hooked" by it. P.D. Wodehouse stated it well when he said, "A parable is one of those stories in the Bible which sounds at first like a yarn, but keeps something up its sleeve which suddenly pops up and knocks you flat."[4] One other definition should suffice. Prentice Meador, Jr. wrote, "A parable then, is a point of comparison between an accepted truth in the reality of the natural world and a new, similar truth in the reality of the spiritual world."[5] As one studies the parables, it becomes clear that Jesus' audiences often found themselves "hooked" by the Lord as He expounded on their misdeeds. A parable represents things as they *are* or as they *could* be, and thus they are always up-to-date in their messages.

The Need for Studying the Parables. The parables of Jesus have often been misunderstood. Throughout the history of Christianity, there have been many forms of interpretation, some of which either limit or mislead us regarding the intended meaning of the Scriptures. Some have tried to make the parables literal in every detail. This is not only wrong, but to make them literal can also cause many problems. A good example of this is the Parable of the Shrewd Manager, in which a man used less than honest means to obtain his ends. But the man's methodology was not the object. Jesus was trying to teach an altogether different message. Others have tried to use the parables as "proof texts" for various doctrines. Again, the purpose of the parables was not to *prove* certain doctrinal matters, even though a correct understanding of them would not contradict biblical teachings. The parables are really illustrations of life in action. The events described in the parables are taken, as it were, from the "trenches" where all of us are working and living.

The parables deal with the very substance of Jesus' teachings. As was pointed out earlier, they address four major themes of Jesus' teachings: *sin, submission, servanthood, and salvation.* You might want to refer to page 16 where this is discussed earlier in a little more detail. Within this context, I suggest that, when the believer in Christ needs to find spiritual strength and sustenance, the parables may very well provide for those deep needs. So, go to them in your time of need. Much of what Jesus taught is right there in those intriguing stories! You do not need to rely only on what Paul *said* Jesus taught; you can read what the Lord Himself said as recorded by those who actually heard Him speak.

The parables are for revelation, not for moralization. Again, this statement does not deny the moral elements of the parables. It simply says that the parables serve as one of God's great means of revelation. Most of the parables show us who God is and how He works in our lives. They often also show us who we are as we relate to God's will. For Jesus telling of the "Good" Samaritan in response to the lawyer shows how humankind relates to God's will. Even though the parables do not distinctly focus on "moralization," there are certainly great moral lessons which may be discerned from the parables. As a matter of fact, the "Learning to Live" section near the end of each chapter is an application of the parables to our everyday life. Even so, a constant attempt is made throughout this study to understand the parables within their context.

The parables of Jesus are certainly unique. I have read many interpretations of the parables so much that many statements almost seem like my own. If I have inadvertently used others' words rather than my own, I apologize. I suggest four important characteristics of the parables: (1) *Jesus' parables tell us much about the great storyteller Himself.* This is certainly true of many writers, speakers, and storytellers. We learn much about their philosophy of life and character by paying attention to what they have written or said. Jesus clearly shows us His concept of the meaning of life through His parables. (2) *Jesus' parables dealt with real life situations*. This is one of the differences between parables and fables. All of the parables are either true or could be true. They are believable. (3) *Jesus' parables attempted to produce a response in the listeners*. Jesus brought *life*. Everything He said and did was for the purpose of helping us understand who we are and what our purpose in life is. (4) *Jesus' parables were simple enough for the simple people and sublime enough for the most intellectual*. They have charmed the reader and enthralled the thinker for nearly 2000 years and it is a safe assertion that they will continue to enlighten the simple and confound the wise for as long as the world stands.

Interpreting the Parables

Understanding the Bible. Hermeneutics, or the methods by which one interprets the Bible, is an ancient topic. In the church of the first three centuries, there developed two major hermeneutical approaches: one was known as the Antiochian approach, and the other was the Alexandrian approach. The Antiochian approach, also known as the historical method, addressed the study of the Bible from a contextual standpoint. The Alexandrian approach, on the other hand, was more of an allegorical method. While the historical method tried to see the Bible from the point of view of how the writer must have intended the message to be understood in keeping with the environmental and social context, the allegorical approach interpreted the Bible as though much of the content of the Scriptures was figurative in nature.

Through the years, many misconceptions have arisen.

Some, wishing to divorce themselves from erroneous methods of understanding the Scriptures, have claimed, "I do not interpret the Bible; I just let it speak for itself." This is a very simplistic way to approach the problem; for, when we read the Bible, we cannot avoid "interpreting" it. Because we *understand* the meaning of the words that we read, we, in fact, interpret them.

As was said earlier, the Bible "is so simple that even a child can understand it." It is true that a child can understand much of it, but it is a mistake for us to infer that a child can understand all of the Bible. There are many deep, overwhelming concepts in Scripture, and some of the ablest scholars through the centuries have struggled over the difficult-to-understand passages. So, it is not that simple. One of the amazing aspects concerning the Bible is that it is simple enough to enthrall the child, but challenging enough to confound the scholar.

Some have claimed that people are dishonest or ignorant who do not understand the Scriptures in the same way that their own particular group or they themselves understand the Bible. Earlier in my own life, I was subjected to this concept. But it did not take long to learn, while sitting at the feet of some of the world's great Biblical scholars, that though I disagreed with them on some matters, they were neither ignorant nor dishonest. The Christian student should search diligently to understand the Scriptures, but one should avoid becoming judgmental of those who do not see the Scriptures alike. This is not meant to suggest that we should give up struggling for the correct answers nor that we should become gullible and immediately believe any doctrine we may hear. We should, as the Bereans, examine "the Scriptures every day to see if what Paul [or someone else] said was true" (Acts 17:11).

In his exploration of the parables, Prentice Meador in his book, *Who Rules Your Life?"* discusses nine characteristics of parables. I encourage you to read his book for a discussion of these characteristics, but for the sake of brevity, they will merely be listed here.

1. The parables of Jesus are essentially oral.
2. The parables of Jesus have a single message.
3. The parables of Jesus can be grouped along certain themes.
4. Jesus intersects real life with his parables.
5. The parables of Jesus are swords that sometimes penetrate the lifestyles of people.
6. The parables of Jesus are brief.
7. The parables of Jesus are permanent.
8. Jesus draws his images from daily experience.
9. The parables of Jesus are not original.[6]

These are very worthwhile statements about Jesus' parables, and each of them could be discussed in much detail. Give special thought to them as you prepare to study and understand the parables of Jesus.

Some Principles for Understanding the Parables. In our study, we will be more interested in studying the parables from the historical, or Antiochian, method of interpretation. I believe that these were lifelike stories which Jesus told to teach specific truths to his listeners. As we prepare to study, the following five "rules" are suggested.

1. As a rule, do not look for deep, dark mysteries in the parables. Jesus was not trying to confound His listeners by telling the parables. In Matthew 13:11–15, Jesus is not saying that He wants the people to misunderstand; but, rather those who do not want to know the truth will not learn it through the parables. Remember that the parables were for the common folk, not for philosophers or theologians to argue about.

2. Learn as much as you can about the scriptural setting of the parable being studied. Usually, this is easy for one to learn from the surrounding text. Jesus often speaks very explicitly concerning the surrounding events.

3. Learn the social contexts of the various events in the parable. There are many social customs prevalent in Jesus' time that are totally foreign to us. Wedding customs, methods of farming, and methods of practicing hospitality are only a few of them. In this study, effort will be given to including as many of the social customs as we can to understand the social contexts of the events being studied.

4. Look for the central lesson of each parable. Most, if not all, of the parables were given for a specific purpose. Often Jesus tells His purpose; sometimes the inspired writers tell us; then, other times it may be a little more difficult. But you must search for the central lesson of the parable. However, do not discount the fact that secondary lessons may be gleaned from the text. Many of these will be discussed in each study in the section "Learning to Live from this Parable." In this, we will often be looking at the parable's present-day application to us. R.C. Trench wrote,

> It will help us much in this matter of determining what is essential and what not, if we first obtain fast hold of the central truth which the parable would set forth, and distinguish it in the mind as accurately as we can from all truths which border upon it; for only as seen from that middle point will the different parts appear in their true light."[7]

5. Interpret the parables as life-learning situations rather than as doctrinal-learning situations. I have emphasized that the focus of this book is "Learning to Live." As we study, a constant effort needs to be exerted to see the life-centeredness of the parables, rather than trying to create or substantiate doctrinal ideas. Again, Trench comments that "the parables

are not to be made first sources of doctrine. Doctrines otherwise grounded may be illustrated, or even further confirmed by them; but it is not allowable to constitute doctrines first by their aid."[8]

Some Problems Faced in Studying the Parables. Most of the problems we face in studying the parables tend to be "self-created." We must exercise great care to avoid falling into some natural traps. The parables can be a *rich* source of Christian strength, but incorrectly used, they can become very troublesome. I want to suggest three problems:

The first problem is our "unwillingness" to look for the real meaning intended. Many of us were "weaned" on studying the Scriptures. We are not consciously aware that we all bring our own agenda to our study of the Bible. Because of this, we may be inclined to interpret a given parable the way we have always heard it interpreted, without giving any thought to its meaning ourselves. Spend time thinking through the parable. Certainly, the meaning you have always heard may be true; but you should approach a study of the Bible with the intent to *learn*, not just reinforce what you already (think you) know.

The second problem we face is our "inability" to set ourselves in Jesus' environment. We are living nearly 2,000 years this side of the events Jesus is describing. For example, what does "a sower went forth to sow" mean to one living in the inner city who may have never seen a field? Or, from the point of view of our modern crime-ridden streets and highways, as well as the legal problems involved in interfering with peoples' lives, why would the Samaritan place the injured man on his beast and take him to the inn to be cared for? We might call the paramedics or the police, but many would hesitate to do what he did. We must understand the environment of Jesus' day.

Finally, a third problem we face in studying the parables is that our media-centered society influences us greatly in our perception of images. We live in a television-centered world; the producers actually create our images for us. This is not so true for reading. As we read these familiar stories of Jesus, we create images for ourselves. Take care in your study that you are not influenced by our media-controlled society as you interpret the images Jesus is giving us.

Arrangement of the Parables

As one reads the many books that have been written on the parables of Jesus, it becomes apparent that there is a difference of opinion on both how many parables there actually are, as well as how they are categorized. These differences of opinion arise from a number of reasons: which sayings of Jesus are actually parables, and which are other types of figures of speech; how various writers feel regarding the subject matter at hand; and a host of other reasons.

I am convinced that there are over 30 parables (probably 30–35, depending on which ones we include). In this study, we will be examining 31 parables. I have chosen to divide them into four major categories: Kingdom Parables, Discipleship Parables; Growth Parables; and Warning and Reward Parables. Some of the parables will be studied together because they are so closely related to each other.

This volume, as stated in the Preface, is the fulfillment of nearly 50 years of my life. It is my sincere hope that our study will be as exciting and fulfilling to you as it has been and will continue to be for me. May God be praised through the study of His word.

Endnotes to Introduction

[1] The New International Version of the Bible is used throughout this study except when otherwise stated.

[2] Neil R. Lightfoot, *The Parables of Jesus*, Part I (Austin, TX: R. B. Sweet Co., Inc., 1963), p. 1.

[3] Edward Hayes Plumptre, "Parable," *Dr. William Smith's Dictionary of the Bible*, ed. H.B. Hackett (Boston: Houghton, Mifflin and Co., 1870), Vol. III, p. 2328.

[4] P.D. Wodehouse, quoted in Archibald M. Hunter, *The Parables Then and Now* (Philadelphia: Westminster, 1971), p. 10.

[5] Prentice A. Meador, Jr., *Who Rules Your Life? Exploring the Kingdom Parables of Jesus* (Austin, TX: Journey Books, 1979), p. 11.

[6] *Ibid.*, pp. 14–19.

[7] Richard Chenevix Trench, *Notes on the Parables of Our Lord*, Popular Edition (Grand Rapids: Baker, 1948), p. 16.

[8] Meador, *Who Rules Your Life?* p. 17.

PART I: PARABLES OF THE KINGDOM

The kingdom was central in the life and teachings of Jesus. When John the Baptist came teaching, he preached that the kingdom of heaven was near (Matt. 3:1–2). After John gave way to the preaching of Jesus, then Jesus "began to preach, 'Repent, for the kingdom of heaven is near'" (Matt. 4:17). From that time forward, Jesus centered His life and message around the kingdom of heaven, or the kingdom of God.

The kingdom was discussed frequently in the parables of Jesus. In a sense, one could state with accuracy that all of the parables taught about the kingdom. But, as we have stated in the introduction to this study, we have divided the parables of Jesus into four types, one of which we call "Parables of the Kingdom." It is in this context that we will be looking at the kingdom — as it is specifically discussed by certain parables.

What was the kingdom in the teachings of Jesus? This topic alone could fill a volume. Many have undertaken the task of defining the term kingdom. Two contrasting definitions will be presented: one by J. Dwight Pentecost and one by William M. Taylor. These two definitions represent two extreme positions concerning the subject. Pentecost wrote,

It is to be stressed that when Christ revealed truth about the kingdom, He was not speaking about the church. When he spoke of the coming kingdom age, he was not speaking of the church age. . . . The coming kingdom age of which Christ spoke began at the time of Israel's rejection of Him as Messiah and will continue until

29

Israel's future reception of Him as the Messiah at the Second
Advent. . . .[1]

There is more than one assumption of the above quotation
that I do not agree with; but, the one we are most interested in
is his statement that the church is not related to Jesus' view of
the kingdom. A quotation more near the view of this author is
that given by Taylor:

> That subject is "the kingdom of heaven," by which is meant not
> the glorified state of the future life, but that presently existing
> community of which Christ is the head, and of which is composed
> those whose hearts and lives are subject to him as their sovereign.[2]

The kingdom includes the church, but in my judgment, it
is larger than the church. The church specifically began on
the Day of Pentecost following Jesus' resurrection. But,
surely, God's kingdom existed prior to that time: it included
those of all ages who accepted God into their lives as king,
and all those who now accept His Son Jesus who reigns over
the kingdom.

The kingdom of God was central in Jesus' teachings. In
fact, the Sermon on the Mount may well be a summary of His
kingdom message. Jesus could speak of the kingdom, therefore, with both a historical perspective and an imminent
expectancy. The Jews had long looked with expectancy for
the kingdom. They looked for a time of fullest blessing (see
Isa. 40:10–11). They believed that both material and spiritual
blessings were promised (Ezek. 36:24–30) and that the kingdom would usher in a physical realm of peace and protection
(cf. Isa. 11:6–9).

How did Jesus view the kingdom? He regarded it as God's
rule over humanity (see Matt. 6:33). That rule began with the
inner person (Luke 17:20–21), and it offers full freedom for a
complete surrender of our person to Jesus. Jesus saw the

kingdom both as "being" (that is, as now in existence) but also as "becoming."

Several of the parables may truly be kingdom parables since they highlight the role of the kingdom in the life of the Christian. This first section, therefore, will focus on those parables I believe to be most closely focused on the subject of the kingdom as it relates to lives of all of us.

Endnotes to Part I Introduction

[1] J. Dwight Pentecost, *The Parables of Jesus* (Grand Rapids: Zondervan, 1982), p. 49.

[2] William M. Taylor, *The Parables of Our Saviour* (Grand Rapids: Kregel Publications, 1975), p. 17.

LANDING IN THE RIGHT PLACE
1

The Parable of the Sower:
Matt. 13:1–23; Mark 4:1–25; Luke 8:5–18

That same day Jesus went out of the house and sat by the lake. Such large crowds gathered around him that he got into a boat and sat in it, while all the people stood on the shore. Then he told them many things in parables, saying: "A farmer went out to sow his seed. As he was scattering the seed, some fell along the path, and the birds came and ate it up. Some fell on rocky places, where it did not have much soil. It sprang up quickly, because the soil was shallow. But when the sun came up, the plants were scorched, and they withered because they had no root. Other seed fell among thorns, which grew up and choked the plants. Still other seed fell on good soil, where it produced a crop — a hundred, sixty or thirty times what was sown. He who has ears, let him hear."

The disciples came to him and asked, "Why do you speak to the people in parables?"

He replied, "The knowledge of the secrets of the kingdom of heaven has been given to you, but not to them. Whoever has will be given more, and he will have an abundance. Whoever does not have, even what he has will be taken from him. This is why I speak to them in parables:

"Though seeing, they do not see;
    though hearing, they do not hear or understand.
In them is fulfilled the prophecy of Isaiah:
    " 'You will be ever hearing but never understanding;
        you will be ever seeing but never perceiving.
    For this people's heart has become calloused;
        they hardly hear with their ears,
        and they have closed their eyes.

> Otherwise they might see with their eyes, hear with their
>   ears,
> understand with their hearts
> and turn, and I would heal them.'

But blessed are your eyes because they see, and your ears because they hear. For I tell you the truth, many prophets and righteous men longed to see what you see but did not see it, and to hear what you hear but did not hear it.

"Listen then to what the parable of the sower means: When anyone hears the message about the kingdom and does not understand it, the evil one comes and snatches away what was sown in his heart. This is the seed sown along the path. What was sown on rocky places is the man who hears the word and at once receives it with joy. But since he has no root, he lasts only a short time. When trouble or persecution comes because of the word, he quickly falls away. What was sown among the thorns is the man who hears the word, but the worries of this life and the deceitfulness of wealth choke it, making it unfruitful. But what was sown on good soil is the man who hears the word and understands it. He produces a crop, yielding a hundred, sixty or thirty times what was sown" (Matt. 13:1–23).

I was standing on the western shore of the Sea of Galilee a few years ago, looking up to the traditional site of the Sermon on the Mount. The ruins of Jesus' hometown during his personal ministry were only about a mile to the north. As I stood gazing into the surrounding area, I thought I could almost see "a sower who went forth to sow" walking back and forth across one of the nearby hills. While standing there, my mind pondered the great truths of this story: the Parable of the Sower.

At this juncture in Jesus' personal ministry, there appears to be a decided change in His methodology. Prior to Matthew 13, Jesus' teaching tended to be centered around His attendance at the synagogue. William Barclay remarks that "At the beginning of his ministry we find him teaching in the *synagogues*; but now we find him teaching on the *seashore*."[1]

Prior to this point in Jesus' teaching ministry, He has not used the parable as we know it; but, from this point, the parable becomes a major part of His teaching method (cf. Matt. 13:34). We are not to assume from this statement that Jesus never taught without using a parable; but, on this particular day in His life, He spoke to them only in parables.

The "Parable of the Sower," as Jesus referred to it (Matt. 13:18), is a very important one for a number of reasons. First, *it is one of His best-known parables.* Some believe it should be regarded as the "Parable of the Soils," but I'll refer to it in Jesus' own language. Second, *this parable helps us to focus on the function of parables.* Jesus was asked by His disciples why He spoke in parables, and in His explanation of the parable, He told them that He used parables so that those who wanted to know the truth could understand, while those who did not want to know the truth would not understand. Then He added, "The knowledge of the secrets of the kingdom of heaven has been given to you, but not to them" (Matt. 13:11–15.) Third, *this parable is one of the few that are recorded in all three of the synoptic gospels.* This does not necessarily make it more important than the others but it does show that the disciples must have been greatly impressed by its richness for all of the writers to include it. Fourth, *this is one of seven parables in the thirteenth chapter of Matthew, all of which refer to some aspect of the kingdom of heaven.* Taylor suggests that "these parables were meant to set before us the origin, hindrances, progress, preciousness, and consummation of the kingdom of God among men. . . ."[2] And, fifth, *this is one of a very few of which Jesus explains its meaning.* The disciples asked Him to explain the parable and Jesus, somewhat allegorically, interpreted the meaning to them.

Background Information

It is important in studying the parables for us to consider the setting of each parable, for in many instances, this will reveal to us why Jesus spoke the parable. In the story of the sower, Luke gives us a little insight into its setting. "After this, Jesus traveled about from one town and village to another, proclaiming the good news of the kingdom of God. The Twelve were with him, and also some women who had been cured of evil spirits and diseases: Mary (called Magdalene) from whom seven demons had come out; Joanna the wife of Cuza, the manager of Herod's household; Susanna; and many others. These women were helping to support them out of their own means" (Luke 8:1–3).

Large crowds were following Him, and Jesus evidently used this opportunity to teach all of them. With the crowds pressing Him, He entered a boat and moved off shore so He could be heard. It is highly possible that Jesus saw and pointed to a sower nearby. Whether this is true or not, it is important for us to see this incident within its context.

The "sowing of seed" needs to be looked at from the ancient world's view of sparce agriculture and not from our world of plenty and our use of massive farming machinery. Although we may have some difficulty identifying with the scene, Jesus' hearers identified with it readily, for it was commonplace. The seeding process was much different from that in our great agricultural belt. Sowing in that ancient land often preceded the plowing: the seeds were often sown and followed by the plowing, which served to cover the seeds.

There were at least two methods of sowing the seed: casting with the hand and letting animals carry bags of seeds on their backs. In the casting with the hand, the sower walked back and forth across the fields, scattering the seeds as he went. In the other method mentioned, bags of seeds were punctured, and the bags were placed on an animal's back. The animal, by walking back and forth across the field, would spread the seeds as it went.

Jesus identified four types of soil: wayside (a trodden path), rocky ground (more likely a rock layer with a thin layer of soil on top), thorny (weedy) ground, and good soil. As one travels in present-day Israel, all of these types of soil are easily visible. These soils were, of course, well-known to the farmers of that day. Using either of the methods of seeding mentioned above, it is easy to see that deliberate placing of seeds in the best places for germination and growing would be next to impossible. It is in this setting that Jesus taught the lessons about the sower.

This parable, along with the parables concerned with the tares, mustard seed, and the yeast, was delivered to the large crowd that had pressed Jesus, causing Him to enter the boat and speak from the edge of the Sea of Galilee. However, the other parables in this chapter — those of the hidden treasure, the pearl of great price, and the dragnet — appear to have been given to the Twelve alone. After the parables of the mustard seed and the yeast, Matthew states that "Jesus spoke all these things to the crowd in parables; he did not say anything to them without using a parable" (Matt. 13:34). And Matthew further explains that "Then he left the crowd and went into the house" (Matt. 13:36). Matthew is careful to relate Jesus' actions as fulfillment of prophecy, and states that this day of parable-speaking "fulfilled what was spoken through the prophet: 'I will open my mouth in parables, I will utter things hidden since the creation of the world'" (Matt. 13:35).

Explaining the Text

The language of this parable is fairly straightforward.

However, there are three expressions that may be clarified by more carefully analyzing their language. The first one relates to Jesus' explanation about the rocky soil to the disciples. Jesus notes that the person who is represented by the rocky soil "lasts only a short time." This expression is from the Greek term πρόσκαιρός εστιν, (*proskairos estin*), and literally means "is temporary."

The second expression is found in Jesus' answer to the disciples' question, "Why do you speak to the people in parables?" Jesus replied, "The knowledge of the secrets of the kingdom of heaven has been given to you, but not to them" (Matt. 13:11). The word we want to explain is the word "secrets" of the kingdom. Is Jesus implying that there are secrets about the kingdom that cannot be known? Not at all. The word here is derived from μυστήριον, (*musterion*), and literally means that "which has not been made known." It does not mean that "it is unknowable," as some suggest. Jesus spoke in parables in order that the mysteries *could* be known.

A third expression we need to explain is Jesus' statement concerning those who were not hearing and understanding. Of them, Jesus said, "In them is fulfilled the prophecy of Isaiah." "In them is fulfilled," from ἀναπληροῦται, (*anapleroutai*), literally is "is being fulfilled" (v. 14). In other words, the "fulfillment" is a continuous action in the present tense. This suggests that Jesus' condemnation referred not only to the Jewish audience of His day, but any today who do not listen and comprehend His teaching are also condemned.

Purpose and Application

This parable was given to impress upon us the need of having an open heart to receive the word which is preached. The title of this chapter is "Landing in the Right Place." By this, I am referring to the seed: it needs to fall upon willing hearts. But, more about this will come in the next section.

The sower in this parable obviously refers to any one who teaches the word to others. It does not, in this usage, refer specifically to Christ. Any preacher or teacher who shares God's word is the sower. The four soils refer to the receivers of the word. It is an awesome responsibility to be a teacher. James wrote, "Not many of you should presume to be teachers, my brothers, because you know that we who teach will be judged more strictly" (James 3:1). Preachers and teachers surely realize that their messages often fall upon deaf ears, and for many, this becomes a great burden. I once knew a wonderfully talented preacher who stopped his full-time preaching role and directed his life into a different kind of Christian service. When asked why he "quit the pulpit," he replied, "I got so discouraged preaching my heart out in the pulpit and seeing nothing happen in the pew."

The primary responsibility of the sower is to sow the seed. We cannot know the condition of the hearts of our listeners. Yet, the seed must be sown. However, this parable teaches that there are varying degrees of hearing or receptivity. Some are not capable of hearing well; others close their minds to hearing. But, whatever the reason, the teacher (or sower) must work diligently to cause his seed to "land right" so that the greatest good can result.

Jesus stressed that *some* seed will spring up, even in the stony and thorny grounds. But the sower's responsibility may not end there. Nurturing is just as important as is sowing. All too often, the cares of the world "choke" it (from θλίψεως, [*thlipseos*], meaning "to press or squeeze, closely akin to tribulation, or to press upon") and it is "unfruitful." Trials and tribulations will come to all of us; but letting the "seed of the kingdom" fall into prepared hearts will help us to remain loyal and faithful.

CHAPTER ONE

"Learning to Live" from this Parable

In our highly industrialized society and scientific agricultural methods, this parable may be difficult for some to
comprehend. In some areas of Los Angeles, California, for
example, there are young people — teens and pre-teens —
who have never seen the Pacific Ocean; yet, they live less
than ten or fifteen miles from the ocean. In large urban areas,
a person can be born, grow up, work and live and die without
ever seeing a seed planted or a crop harvested. Yet, the lesson
Jesus gives for living here is very poignant.

One of the most valuable lessons for living for us to learn
is that *we must take great care that the seed (truth) we plant
falls on willing ears.* When telling our fellow earth-pilgrims
of the story of salvation, we must properly prepare the soil.
To use Jesus' figure, we must take out all of the rocks,
destroy as many of the thorns and weeds as we can, and sow
the seed in receptive hearts. When this is done, we can be
more assured of an abundant harvest of souls. From the
receiver point of view, we must be good listeners lest we miss
the message of the Christ being taught us. We are often so
caught up with what we want or what is popular that we fail
to listen properly. Studies show that the average person
spends more time in listening than in any other kind of
communication. Isn't it marvelous that long before scientific
studies in listening were being conducted, Jesus gave us the
exhortation to listen with open ears.

A second lesson for living from this parable is that *we
should develop patience in our sowing the seed of the kingdom.* For the most part, results do not come quickly. We may
have to sow the seed many times to the same person before
that person is receptive. How often preachers and teachers see
people struggling with the message of truth before they are
ready to accept that truth.

A third lesson for living from this parable is that *we are not "soil inspectors."* We simply sow the seeds without making judgments about the soil. How do we know a heart is stony or thorny? Our task as Christians is to sow the seed; God will take care of the growth and harvest.

Satan is constantly at work to thwart our efforts to teach the lost. He will do whatever he can to stand in the way of people hearing and accepting the gospel. We must be prepared for whatever hindrances Satan may put in our way of teaching and learning what God wants us to know and do.

Strive to sow the seed in the most likely places for growth and pray for the seed to fall in the good soil. Our lives and the lives of those whom we may influence may bring forth an abundant harvest. Remember that "what was sown on good soil is the man who hears the word and understands it. He produces a crop, yielding a hundred, sixty or thirty times what was sown" (Matt. 13:23). Each of us will produce abundantly and in comparison to the abilities each of us has to serve.

Endnotes for Chapter 1

[1] William Barclay, *The Gospel of Matthew*, Revised Edition (Philadelphia: Westminster, 1975), Vol. II, p. 53.

[2] Taylor, *The Parables of Our Saviour*, p. 18.

BIG THINGS IN LITTLE PACKAGES
2

The Parable of the Growing Seed: Mark 4:26–29

He also said, "This is what the kingdom of God is like. A man scatters seed on the ground. Night and day, whether he sleeps or gets up, the seed sprouts and grows, though he does not know how. All by itself the soil produces grain — first the stalk, then the head, then the full kernel in the head. As soon as the grain is ripe, he puts the sickle to it, because the harvest has come" (Mark 4:26–29).

The period of history in which we are living is often referred to as the "Post-Christian Era." There are many reasons for this. During the 20th century, humanism (the philosophy that human beings are the center of everything) has become a very dominant force. Religion is still with us, but many people attempt to make religion fit their mold rather than fitting religion's mold.

Jesus demanded that He have first place or no place in the lives of His followers (cf. Matt. 16:24). This has caused a great deal of consternation in the minds of professing Christians. How can I put Christ first and still be successful? Don't I have a right to do what *I* want to do? If I am not at the center of my life, how can I climb whatever ladder that I am trying to climb? These and other questions haunt many in our generation.

Christianity in America has lost much of its captivating power. C. Leonard Allen addressed this issue when he wrote,

One of the chief characteristics of modern secular culture is the loss of this sense of connectedness to the past. The spirit of individualness, rampant in our time, says: "You can be whatever you choose to be. Forget the past. Disregard its traditions. Dismiss its stories. Accept none of its constraints. Bear no responsibilities for its failures. For you are perfectly free to order your own life, to go your own way."[1]

This is not a new problem. During the last half of the first century, Christians were asking why Jesus had not returned. "Has He failed to fulfill the mission of God?" they asked. "Have we believed in vain?"

Today, many are asking, "If Jesus brought the kingdom, why has it not been more successful? If the kingdom of God is the most powerful force in the world, why are people not flocking to it? Why isn't it growing more?" The apostles, the early Christians, and we today are often impatient with the way God brings about growth. This brief parable addresses this question, and Jesus gives us some of the answer in the parable. Perhaps the simplicity of the parable influences us to totally miss the purpose of it.

Background Information

Our present parable is found only in Mark's Gospel. It is the only parable that is found in Mark alone. Mark gave it along with the parables of the Sower and of the Mustard Seed, which leads us to believe that He delivered this on the same occasion. In fact, after the end of these parables, Mark states, "With many similar parables Jesus spoke the word to them, as much as they could understand. He did not say anything to them without using a parable" (Mark 4:33–34). So, since the background information would be the same for the Parable of the Sower and this parable, you should look back to the previous chapter for this background information.

Some writers suggest that this parable is a sequel to the

Parable of the Sower, and Taylor says that it "was designed to complete the history of the growth of the good seed which fell on the good ground."[2] A.B. Bruce states that this parable "is a pendant to the parable of the Sower, teaching that even in the case of the fourth type of hearers [those represented by the "good soil"] the production of fruit is a gradual process demanding time."[3]

Explaining the Text

As is indicated earlier, this parable is found only in the Gospel of Mark; however, it seems to be intimately related to other parables that are recorded particularly by Matthew. Since it is such a brief parable, there are fewer textual problems or items of interest. We are not certain whether this parable was spoken to the large crowd that was gathered by the Sea of Galilee or whether it was given only to Jesus' closest circle of followers, His apostles. Mark simply says, "He also said . . ." (Mark 4:26).

To those who have not had an agrarian life, this parable may not have the meaning that it would for those who have planted and watched plants grow. What Jesus is describing here is the natural process of a seed's development into a mature, fruit-producing plant. Jesus obviously knew how plants grow and understood that it takes time for the plant to be fully useful. In order to conform to nature, a plant has a normal pattern or procedure for its growth process.

One other term needs to be explained. The text says that "*All by itself* (emphasis mine) the soil produces. . . ." (Mark 4:28). This expression is a translation of the Greek word αὐτομάτη (*automate*), and it is used only here and in Acts 12:10. It means "self-acting" and is the word from which we get our English word "automatic." What Jesus is saying here is that the seed did what it was expected to do; it acted on its own. It did what it was made to do — grow! Perhaps there may be a hint here that we should do what we are expected to do as followers of the Lord. The thrust of the text of the parable, therefore, is to specify the gradual growth of the seed into its full and mature stage.

Purpose and Application

The primary purpose of this parable is to show how the kingdom of God grows. It is often a silent and unobserved growth. To those of us who are impatient, this parable is saying, "Don't give up on God. He will accomplish His purpose in His own good time."

When I was a young minister, I often became very discouraged when people did not accept Christ as quickly as *I* thought they should. After all, I had taught them the truth. Why couldn't they understand it and obey? I knew that Paul had written, "I planted the seed, Apollos watered it, but God made it grow" (1 Cor. 3:6). But, you see, *I* was trying to take over God's job. *God* makes the seed grow. Know for a certainty that the seed *can* and *will* progress; in fact, it will progress many times even though we do not do our job. But, if we will do our job of planting the seed, God will make it grow.

There is another interesting thing about planting and reaping. It seems like weeds grow all by themselves. Have you ever planted weeds in your garden intentionally? Weeds seem to grow by themselves. But, if we want good plants to grow, we must plant *good* seed.

A second application of this parable is that *the kingdom grows best when it does so gradually.* Sudden or rapid growth often involves bypassing some of the necessary stages of growth that are essential for stability. One example of this in the early church was the practice of "mass baptisms." After

Christianity became legal, following the time of Constantine the Great, often whole armies would be "baptized" together. When the leader of the military unit was converted to Christianity, he often bestowed "salvation" on all of his soldiers. This was beneficial for those "counting noses." Sure, the number of "Christians" was growing. However, they were bypassing one of the vital ingredients to a wholesome conversion: teaching. By the beginning of the Middle Ages, the "Christians" did not have a doctrinal foundation on which to stand. When the Moslem religion began to take the world, many "Christians" were converted to Islam. Why? Because they did not have depth of soil: they had not learned the doctrinal underpinnings of Christianity. It is a much healthier church that grows gradually, because it can develop the needed strength to remain faithful to Christ when the times are tough.

The kingdom best grows when the growth is ordered. In this parable, Jesus delineates the order of growth of the seeds: "first the stalk, then the head, then the full kernel in the head" (Mark 4:28). This is the way that the seed ought to grow. Sometimes, we try to baptize people before we teach them. We must plant the seed into hearts, let the seed germinate, water and care for the plants as they grow, then give encouragement to the fledgling Christian. Only if we allow people to grow in the proper order can we be assured that they have really learned the truth about Jesus.

"Learning to Live" from this Parable

This parable is indeed rich in meaning. We can learn so much about the nature of the growth of the kingdom and about the growth of our own lives if we listen to what Jesus is saying.

We must not be overly concerned about growth if we have

properly sown the seed. It is not our task to provide the growth. In fact, we are incapable of making anything grow. We are totally dependent on God for growth. Paul wrote, "I planted the seed, Apollos watered it, but God made it grow. So neither he who plants nor he who waters is anything, but only God, who makes things grow" (1 Cor. 3:6–7). We have very little to do with the actual growth of our fellow-Christians. We can plant, we can water, we can encourage, but God gives the increase. Be patient as you watch others grow. Don't get discouraged if you aren't growing as rapidly as you expect to. We must allow ourselves and others room to grow.

The Kingdom will Grow; God willed it to grow. The growth may not follow the pattern that we have in mind for it. But growth will come, Paul assures us. To the Galatians, he wrote,

> Do not be deceived: God cannot be mocked. A man reaps what he sows. The one who sows to please his sinful nature, from that nature will reap destruction; the one who sows to please the Spirit, from the Spirit will reap eternal life. Let us not become weary in doing good, for at the proper time we will reap a harvest if we do not give up (Gal. 6:7–9).

There is no place for the faint-hearted. There is no room for discouragement. God *will* provide growth.

There are a number of lessons that we can learn from this short parable. (1) *We can learn about the complexity of growth.* It is difficult for mortals to know exactly how growth takes place. Sure, the scientist can explain the process of growth and what makes a plant or a person grow. But it still remains a mystery. What was it that took a man like Peter, who was so impetuous, and prepared him to write such a magnificent epistle as 1 Peter? Jesus, in talking about the complexity of growth, said, ". . . the seed sprouts and grows, though he does not know how" (Mark 4:27). Nor do we really know how. But, just because we don't understand *how* the seed works, we don't quit sowing. I plant a garden every year, but I don't know how or why it produces as it does. Yet, I don't quit planting a garden just because I do not understand what makes it grow a certain way.

(2) *We see the gradualness of growth.* Jesus said, "Night and day, whether he sleeps or gets up . . ." (Mark 4:27). We cannot actually see the growth of a plant, but it is growing nonetheless. You don't plant a seed and then sit watching for it to germinate and grow. Nor can you see growth. It takes place at its own rate of speed. In the same way, we cannot rush the growth of ourselves or of fellow-Christians.

(3) *There are stages of growth.* As stated earier, there is an order to growth and development. If you are planting corn, the ear does not fully develop prior to its forming a tassle on the top of the plant. Nor does an orange tree produce fruit before it has blossomed. There is an order. Jesus said that the seed "produces grain — first the stalk, then the head, then the full kernel in the head" (Mark 4:28). Not until it has advanced through these stages does the plant actually produce the ripened fruit or grain. So also in the life of a Christian. We must make way for people to go through the stages of growth.

God's word will not return to Him void. It will produce fruit. It will bring about change in the lives of men and women who hear it. It will grow at different speeds with different people; but it will grow. Pray to God that, as we see the growth that God's sickle will harvest us into His eternal kingdom.

Endnotes for Chapter 2

[1] C. Leonard Allen, *The Cruciform Church: Becoming a Cross-Shaped People in a Secular World* (Abilene, TX: ACU Press, 1990), pp. 2–3.

[2] Taylor, *The Parables of Our Saviour*, p. 196

[3] Alexander Balmain Bruce, "The Synoptic Gospels," in *The Expositor's Greek Testament*, edited by W. Robertson Nicoll (London: Hodder and Stoughton, 1912), Vol. I, pp. 367–368.

SATAN'S EVIL IN GOD'S WORLD
3

The Parable of the Tares: Matt. 13:24–30; 36–44

Jesus told them another parable: "The kingdom of heaven is like a man who sowed good seed in his field. But while everyone was sleeping, his enemy came and sowed weeds among the wheat, and went away. When the wheat sprouted and formed heads, then the weeds also appeared.

"The owner's servants came to him and said, 'Sir, didn't you sow good seed in your field? Where then did the weeds come from?'

" 'An enemy did this,' he replied.

"The servants asked him, 'Do you want us to go and pull them up?'

" 'No,' he answered, 'because while you are pulling the weeds, you may root up the wheat with them. Let both grow together until the harvest. At that time I will tell the harvesters: First collect the weeds and tie them in bundles to be burned, then gather the wheat and bring it into my barn'" (Matt. 13:24–30).

. . . Then he left the crowd and went into the house. His disciples came to him and said, "Explain to us the parable of the weeds in the field."

He answered, "The one who sowed the good seed is the Son of Man. The field is the world, and the good seed stands for the sons of the kingdom. The weeds are the sons of the evil one, and the enemy who sows them is the devil. The harvest is the end of the age, and the harvesters are the angels.

"As the weeds are pulled up and burned in the fire, so it will be at the end of the age. The Son of Man will send out his angels, and they will weed out of his kingdom everything that causes sin and all who do evil. They will throw them into the fiery furnace, where there will be weeping and gnashing of teeth. Then the righteous will shine like

the sun in the kingdom of their Father. He who has ears, let him hear" (Matt. 13:36–44).

The story is told in my hometown that a local funeral director had replanted the front lawn of the funeral home with a beautiful grass. During the night, one of his friends, a prominent businessman, sowed turnips in the lawn as a mischievous prank on his friend. Not to be outdone, after the turnips had matured, the funeral director responded by setting up a stand in the front of the funeral home and selling the turnips to passers-by.

As I said, this was done as a friendly prank. But the story that Jesus tells in Matthew 13 was not conceived as a prank. This was an attack of Satan, the prince of evil, upon a man seeking to do right. This parable is one of grave importance to us. How does God deal with evil among the righteous?

Background Information

You will notice that throughout this chapter, we refer to this as "The Parable of the Tares." In most earlier translations, the word "weeds" in the NIV was translated by the word "tares." Note the discussion in the next section. Furthermore, this parable is often studied in conjunction with the Parable of the Dragnet. Taylor observes that

> these two parables [the Tares and the Dragnet] must be taken together. . . . Both alike deal with the co-existence of good and evil within the same enclosure, and both of them look at the question of the absolute separation of the evil from the good; but the one gives prominence to the impracticability of attaining that before a certain period, while the other emphasizes the assurance that such a separation will be ultimately secured.[1]

Neil Lightfoot also believes that these two parables ought to be studied together, for he says that "both of them deal with the coexistence of good and evil, and both teach that, although good and evil may stand side by side for awhile, eventually a great and permanent separation will be made between them."[2]

It is true that both parables have to do with the separation of the good from the evil, but because they seem to be focused differently, they will be examined separately in our study. There is also an affinity between the Parable of the Sower and this parable; however, their kinship arises from the fact that both parables use the sowing of seed as one of the prime elements of the story.

The setting of this parable is generally believed to be the same as that of the Parable of the Sower and others delivered in Matthew 13.[3] It appears that the parable was spoken at the time of seeding of the fields. The situation is at the western shore of the Sea of Galilee where Jesus has gotten in a boat due to the press of the crowds and was speaking to the large crowd from the boat. Within this context, Matthew presents the parable as being one of a number of parables that Jesus delivered. One further observation is that this parable is only given by Matthew.

Again, this is a very familiar scene for the people there. Whereas in the Parable of the Sower, we see the sower sowing the seed, in this parable the seeds have already been sown, but an enemy has sown wild seeds among those sown by the farmer. The nature of these seeds will be discussed in the next section. A.B. Bruce observes that the Parable of the Sower "describes past experiences; the *Tares* is prophetic of a future state of things."[4]

This parable presents us with some problems. The problem of evil is a constantly perplexing one. Why would God allow evil to grow in the midst of the good? If God is a loving God, some ask, then why does He not protect His people from the presence of evil? Has God allowed Satan complete free reign over the world? Can Satan sow his wicked seeds anywhere he wants to? Again, others see this parable as opposing any kind of church discipline. Do church leaders not have a right to remove evil influences from the within the church? These and other questions have made this parable a rather difficult one for us to understand. Some of these questions will be answered in the following pages; but, of course, some questions regarding evil and its power over us may not be completely answered while we are fettered by the flesh.

Explaining the Text

This parable has two peculiarities which few others have. First, it is one of the few parables that Jesus explained to His disciples. Second, it *sounds* like an analogy, and in Jesus' explanation of it, He speaks as though it were an analogy: each part has its own corresponding meaning. But Jesus called it a parable, and it does have the flavor of a parable as one reads it.

One of the distinct differences of this parable from others is Jesus' use of the word "tares," as it is translated in most English texts. The Greek word here is ζιζάνιον (*zizanion*), which refers to a weed called "cheat" or "darnel." As was stated earlier, the more common word used in earlier English translations is "tares." Darnel was a very troublesome weed in ancient Palestine. Barclay has this interesting comment:

> The tares and the wheat are so like each other that the Jews called the tares *bastard wheat*. Hebrew for tares is *zunim*, whence comes the Greek *zizanion*; *zunim* is said to be connected with the word *zanah*, which means *to commit fornication*; and the popular story is that the tares took their origin in the time of wickedness which preceded the flood, for at that time the whole creation, men, animals and plants, all went astray, and committed fornication and brought forth contrary to nature. In their early stages the wheat

and the tares so closely resembled each other that the popular idea
was that the tares were a kind of wheat which had gone wrong.[5]

Whether the above statement is true or not, we do know that
the tares (or, darnel) looked very much like wheat when it
was young, but it was a very troublesome weed. Some have
suggested that it may have been somewhat poisonous.
Buttrick wrote that "Darnel is false wheat, hard to distinguish
from the real grain, and poisonous to eat."[6]

Purpose and Application

Earlier, we stated that this parable is thought by some to
eliminate any kind of church discipline. We know this is not
true, for there are a number of instances in Scripture where
we are told to exercise discipline. In 1 Corinthians 5:5, Paul
told the Corinthians, regarding the man who was living with
his father's wife, "hand this man over to Satan, so that the
sinful nature may be destroyed and his spirit saved on the day
of the Lord." Matthew records Jesus saying that if a brother
refuses to listen when he is appropriately reproved, we are to
"tell it to the church; and if he refuses to listen even to the
church, treat him as you would a pagan or a tax collector"
(Matt. 18:17). These and other scriptural admonitions tell us
that we *should* exercise discipline within the church. But,
what does this parable say to us?

First, *the kingdom, or church, must exist in the presence of
evil.* Evil is all around us. We cannot avoid the presence of
evil, but we do not have to become involved with evil.
Someone has said, "You can't keep the birds from flying over
your head; but you can keep them from making nests in your
hair." When we are born again, we separate ourselves from
the life of sin and become slaves of Christ. The wheat often
has to remain with the tares until the time of the harvest.

Second, *God permits humanity to live wickedly until the*

55

harvest. It is tempting for us to wish that there were no evil influences we had to fight against. But then our obedience would not be from choice but by constraint. We would be obeying God because He gave us no choice. God has made us to be free moral agents. We make our own choices. We can choose to obey God, or we can choose to reject Him. We can live as wickedly as we please until death.

Third, *both the wicked and the righteous will live together until the harvest.* Almost from the beginning of the Christian era, many have tried to escape evil by becoming hermits or ascetics. This is not the answer. Jesus did not tell us to escape the world but to live in it. "My prayer is not that you take them out of the world but that you protect them from the evil one. They are not of the world, even as I am not of it" (John 17:15–16). Christians must learn how to cope with living in the presence of evil without becoming contaminated by its evils.

Fourth, *there will be a day of reckoning.* The harvest is coming when the tares, or weeds, will be separated from the wheat, when the evil will be separated from the good. Then will God reward those of His servants who have been loyal to His Son's covenant. Some religious people have discounted the fact of a day of reckoning, or a day of judgment. Jesus declares that it is a fact. See Matthew 25:31–46.

"Learning to Live" from this Parable

One of the great themes which persists in this parable is the way we deal with evil as it relates to the other person. Jesus admonished that the tares, or weeds, not be pulled up because "you may root up the wheat with them" (Matt. 13:29). Paul is also mindful of the weaker brother as he is admonished to turn from sin. "Brothers, if someone is caught in a sin, you who are spiritual should restore him gently"

(Gal. 6:1). Thus, some of the ways we can give this parable meaning in our lives involve learning how to deal with wrong without damaging the one who is involved in the sin.

We should season our criticism of others with love and with caution. It is very easy for us to let ourselves be placed in the position of judging. Scripture constantly admonishes us to avoid such a position. Jesus admonished us to "stop judging by mere appearances, and make a righteous judgment" (John 7:24). In the context of this parable, Jesus is saying to us that if we do not know for sure which is wheat and which is tares or weeds, we should "let them grow together." By treating others fairly and honestly, one might be able to lead the unrighteous to Him who can make him righteous.

We must learn to cope with a world filled with evil. The world with all its charms is a wicked place. Sin is rampant! It would be difficult for one to see the sin and corruption in the world and deny that there is a devil, an evil influence, having a profound effect upon all of us. Remember, Jesus did not want His people taken out of the world; rather, He wanted them to learn to cope with the world. Trying to run from the evil world can be counterproductive. If we are surrounded with Christian support, we can cope with the evil. As long as the world stands, *there will be evil* in the world. We have been promised that we will not be tempted with more than we can endure.

Jesus did not condone the presence of evil, nor should we. When Jesus said "Let both grow together," He was not suggesting to us that evil is to be "winked at," or lightly ignored. On the contrary, Jesus hates sin, but He loves the sinner. I heard someone say recently, "God does not forgive sin; He forgives the sinners." Sin is just as despised in God's eye now as it ever has been. We should not condone the presence of evil. But we should involve ourselves in the eradication of sin. We must let the non-Christian realize that we do not approve of sin.

Often, good plants can be damaged if we deal incorrectly with the bad ones. "Let them grow together till the harvest!" The hearts and lives of many people are so fragile. We must deal with wickedness firmly, but let the sinner know that we love him/her. If a weak person sees us dealing without the spirit of love in our hearts, that weak Christian may be irreparably hurt. Jesus recognized that the spirits of people are so fragile. For this reason, He wants us to treat people with care. As the mailing sticker says about some packages, *"Fragile; Handle with Care."* Many years ago, a preacher friend of mine said, "You have to make people angry in order to convert them." I did not then agree, nor do I agree now. It may be true that a few people will not be led to investigate their lives without being made angry, but I am convinced that this does not represent the majority of people. "Let them grow together until the harvest. At that time I will tell the harvesters; First collect the weeds and tie them in bundles to be burned, then gather the wheat and bring it into my barn" (Matt. 13:30–31).

Endnotes for Chapter 3

[1] Taylor, *The Parables of Our Saviour*, p. 38.

[2] Neil R. Lightfoot, *The Parables of Jesus* (Austin,TX: R.B. Sweet Co., Inc., 1963), p. 42.

[3] There is some difference of opinion concerning whether this parable was delivered on the same occasion as others in Matthew 13. However, the text does not give any reason for questioning this. A.B. Bruce suggests that there is a division of opinion concerning this. See *The Parabolic Teaching of Christ* (New York: A.C. Armstrong and Son, 1908), p. 38.

[4] A.B. Bruce, "The Synoptic Gospels," p. 199.

[5] William Barclay, *The Gospel of Matthew* Vol. II, p. 73.

[6] Buttrick, *The Parables of Jesus* (Grand Rapids: Baker, 1928), p. 63.

FINDING GREAT TREASURES
4

**The Parables of the Hidden Treasure and The Pearl of Great Price:
Matt. 13:44–46**

**"The kingdom of heaven is like treasure hidden in a field. When a
man found it, he hid it again, and then in his joy went and sold all he
had and bought that field.**

**"Again, the kingdom of heaven is like a merchant looking for fine
pearls. When he found one of great value, he went away and sold
everything he had and bought it" (Matt. 13:44–46).**

Can you imagine the feeling experienced by the person
who found the first gold lode in California in 1849? Should
he run and tell someone? Or should he keep the secret to
himself? What was the feeling of those Europeans who first
discovered America? I have often contemplated the wonder-
ment experienced by the first person who gazed into the
Yosemite Valley in California, certainly one of the most beautiful sites in our land. Discovery is a wonderful experience: to
discover a new truth, to learn a new skill, to attain a long-
sought-after goal, or to find a priceless treasure.

Background Information
The parables we turn to now focus on the joy of great
discovery. Although they are given by Jesus as two parables,
they really address almost the same thing. They are similar in
some aspects; they are different in others. But both are
concerned with the great joy one experiences when the king-

dom of heaven is discovered.

Jesus had spent much time with the crowds at the Sea of Galilee. It was perhaps at this time that Jesus began to use the parable as a form of teaching. In Matthew 13:36, we learn that Jesus "left the crowd and went into the house." It was here that Jesus explained to the disciples the Parable of the Tares. It was following this explanation Jesus seems to have spoken the parables we are presently studying. There does not appear to be any content connection between this parable and the others in this same context; it was just spoken on the same occasion as the others were. There is no indication concerning which "house" Jesus entered; perhaps it was Peter's, or maybe the one in which Jesus was living.

These two parables are studied together because they have much in common. Both discuss the price one would pay for a great treasure that was found. Both relate the kingdom of God to the finding of a great treasure. In each of them, the buyer gave all that he had to purchase the new-found treasure.

Some have criticized Jesus concerning this parable. Why would Jesus condone the first man "hiding" the treasure before he went to try to buy it? Isn't this a bit underhanded? Neither of these parables should be interpreted as teaching about a moral issue. This is one of the problems faced when we interpret parables literally, with every detail being applied to the meaning of the parable. Jesus was not concerned in the story with how the treasures were "found" but rather what the finder did upon discovering the treasures. The Lord was trying to teach these learners, His disciples, about the worth of the kingdom of God.

Explaining the Text

The Parable of the Hidden Treasure is certainly a unique parable, and it is burdened with some problems. How does it happen that a man suddenly finds a treasure of inestimable value? Who put it there? Why had he not come back for it? We can only speculate about the answers to these questions. Kistemaker has given this background bearing on these questions:

> A treasure has been hidden in a field. Who put it there and how long ago are questions that cannot be answered. We do know that in ancient Palestine, a country frequently ravished by war, people often hid their treasure or part of it in a field rather than in a house. In a house, thieves would be able to find it; in a field, the treasure would be safe. But if the owner were killed during the war, he would carry his secret with him to the grave, and no one would ever know where he had hidden the treasure.[1]

It may be that this is what happened at this particular time. However, we do know that treasures are still being found buried in houses and other places. Archaeologists have found such treasures repeatedly. Some examples could be cited, such as the "digs" around the Dead Sea Scroll Community and findings in and around Capernaum, to mention only two. Those interested in pursuing this further may read such documents as the *Biblical Archaeological Review* for examples of such finds.

There were no banks, as we know them today, in ancient Palestine. The nearest thing to it might be the money-changers, so prominent in Jesus' day. Victor Matthews wrote that,

> Despite the free use of many different currencies, money changers did exist to exchange foreign coins for the silver didrachma of Tyre which was used to pay the temple tax. A fee was charged for this service of between 4 and 8 percent. They also served as bankers, paying interest on money left in their charge (Mt 25:37).[2]

But banks as we think of them in our day did not exist. I will say more about this when we look at the Parable of the Talents.

The Parable of the Hidden Treasure presents a problem to some readers. Was the man who found the treasure completely honest? Should he not have told the owner that he had found the treasure rather than purchasing it without informing him? Is Jesus condoning dishonesty? Certainly not. The parable is not addressing the issue of how the man found the treasure. There is no moral issue involved here, for the purpose of the parable is not concerned with that. The issue that Jesus is emphasizing here is that the man, although he was not searching for the treasure, *found* it. And *when he found it* he sold all that he had to buy this great treasure. That is the great truth that Jesus is emphasizing. The kingdom of heaven is a priceless treasure: worthy of all we have or can ever attain!

The parable of the priceless pearl involves a connoisseur of fine pearls. He was a merchant seeking fine pearls. Two words related in meaning are ἔμπορος (*emporos*, a wholesale merchant) and καπηλός (*kapelos*, a retail merchant). This man was the former, a wholesale merchant, and he evidently knew what he was looking for. Thus, this merchant did not "chance upon" the priceless pearl; he was diligently searching for it. He was a *seeker* of fine pearls. When he found it, he recognized its value. And, like the man who accidentally found the treasure, he went and sold all he had in order to buy that one pearl.

Purpose and Application

These two parables are among the shortest that Jesus gave; but they explode with meaning. As I have stated earlier, Jesus was not focusing on any moral issues we might see today; rather, He was interested in showing the exquisite worth of the kingdom of God.

The kingdom of heaven is far more valuable than any

sacrifice that we could present for it. Jesus told us that the kingdom of God should have the highest priority in our lives. "But seek first his kingdom and his righteousness, and all these things will be given to you as well" (Matt. 6:33). He also told us that following Him requires that we deny ourselves as a prerequisite to following Him. "Then Jesus said to his disciples, 'If anyone would come after me, he must deny himself and take up his cross and follow me'" (Matt. 16:24). The cost of following Christ as our Savior requires that we give up allegiance to everything else. This is what these two treasure-hunters did: they gave up everything they had to grasp that treasure or that pearl that was so valuable. This is undoubtedly the supreme lesson of this parable.

There are two ways that people learn of the kingdom. Some have just stumbled upon the kingdom. They were not looking for it; they just happened to be in the right place at the right time. I have known some individuals who have attained the kingdom in such a way as this. A woman and her son were passing the church building where I was preaching one Easter Sunday. Thinking it would be the appropriate thing to do, they stopped and came to our worship. After visitation and study with them, both of them became Christians. They had not been searching for the truth; they "just stumbled upon" it. This is illustrated by the man who found the treasure in the field.

Others, however, spend much time and effort seeking God's kingdom before they find it. For some, this becomes a very arduous task. Like the merchant, they search diligently for the kingdom before they indeed find it. I have had students come to me and ask help in their quest for the truth. We have all heard many stories of people seeking the kingdom of God. In truth, this search is the work of a lifetime, for all of us are constantly involved in the pursuit for truth. In the words of Solomon, we should "buy the truth and do not sell it" (Prov. 23:23). Jesus said, "You will know the truth, and the truth will set you free" (John 8:32).

The kingdom of heaven is a very beautiful treasure. We live in a very stained and tarnished world. As I write these words, news of murder and mayhem is all around me. In this current school year, murder is rampant at Los Angeles metropolitan high schools. A Los Angeles newspaper reported four murders on its front page in one day. As we contemplate the sinful world in which we live, is there not something else, something much better? The kingdom of heaven offers us respite from sin.

Paul discussed burial with Christ in baptism (Col. 2:12), then added,

> Since, then, you have been raised with Christ, set your hearts on things above, where Christ is seated at the right hand of God. Set your minds on things above, not on earthly things. For you died, and your life is now hidden with Christ in God. When Christ, who is your life, appears, then you will also appear with Him in glory (Col. 3:1–4).

Paul emphasizes the extraordinary life which we have in Christ Jesus. One of my students told me recently how her total life had changed since she had given her life to Christ. She had not been religious prior to her encounter with Christ which led to her conversion; but Christ changed her total focus. The kingdom of heaven will do this to us. The kingdom is truly a very beautiful treasure — one that is worth our cashing in everything we have in order to possess it.

The only way to possess the kingdom is to sell all. The man who found the treasure sold all to buy his treasure; the pearl merchant sold everything in order to buy that special pearl he discovered! If Christ truly enters our life, we must "sell everything we have." By this, we do not necessarily mean a literal selling; we just must put everything into proper perspective. Jesus must be put first in our lives. Just remember: "Buy the truth and do not sell it!" After showing what he was and had prior to his conversion, Paul wrote, "whatever was to my profit I now consider loss for the sake of Christ. What is more, I consider everything a loss compared to the surpassing greatness of knowing Christ Jesus my Lord. . . . I consider them rubbish, that I may gain Christ . . ." (Phil. 3:7–8).

"Learning to Live" from this Parable

Salvation is at the heart of these gems of wisdom we have been studying. In the kingdom of heaven, there is peace and rest. Israel had longed for the kingdom of God; her prophets had foretold its coming; and in the imagery created in those prophecies of old, there was promise of redemption. Isaiah, after describing the hideous sins of Israel against Jehovah, tells of the coming of a peaceful kingdom (*cf.* Isa. 2:1ff). So, when Jesus told His disciples of the hidden treasure and of the pearl of great price, they must have had glimpses of the kingdom about which they had dreamed. What, then, do these two parables teach us about living in the kingdom?

First, *the kingdom is within reach of all of us.* This was a new order of living than Israel had known. In her relationship with God, only the Israelites were God's special people. Now, the kingdom provides salvation for all humanity. Yes, the kingdom is within reach of all of us, but not without a price. Both of the finders of treasure in these parables gave up everything. Many of us may look at our own position in life and say, "But, I cannot give much; I have but little to give." Others who read these words may have much to give. Regardless of our station in life, *we can give all we have.* That is what Jesus is demanding. The widow and her gift of

65

the two "very small copper coins" represented her gift of everything (see Mark 12:41–44). If we are willing to make the supreme sacrifice of ourselves, God will provide treasures far greater than we can imagine!

Second, *salvation is an individual thing.* Paul admonished the Philippians to "continue to work out your salvation" (Phil. 2:12). I cannot obey God for someone else. I am not a Christian because my parents were. Someone has appropriately said, "God has no grandchildren, only children." I cannot search for others' salvation, and they cannot search for mine. This is an individual responsibility each of us must assume.

Third, *our assessment of the importance of the kingdom may be seen by how much we are really willing to give.* The rich young ruler (see Matt. 19:16–30) was not willing to give everything. When Jesus told him that he should go and sell what he had and give it to the poor, he was not willing to make that sacrifice. However, Jesus assured him that this was what it took for him to enter into the kingdom of heaven. How important is the kingdom to you? Are you willing to "go and sell all you have" for the kingdom? Or is the price too high?

Endnotes for Chapter 4

[1] Simon Kistemaker, *The Parables of Jesus* (Grand Rapids: Baker, 1980), p. 54.

[2] Victor Matthews, *Manner and Customs in the Bible* (Peabody, MA: Hendrickson Publishers, 1988), p. 248.

MEASURING THE CATCH
5

The Parable of the Dragnet: Matt. 13:47–50

"Once again, the kingdom of heaven is like a net that was let down into the lake and caught all kinds of fish. When it was full, the fishermen pulled it up on the shore. Then they sat down and collected the good fish in baskets, but threw the bad away. This is how it will be at the end of the age. The angels will come and separate the wicked from the righteous and throw them into the fiery furnace, where there will be weeping and gnashing of teeth" (Matt. 13:47–50).

Many students of the parables believe that this parable needs to be studied alongside the parable of the tares (recall from an earlier discussion that the NIV uses "weeds" while most other translations use "tares").[1] Others feel that it belongs with the Parables of the Hidden Treasure and the Pearl of Great Price.[2] However, this parable has some very distinctive and unique lessons that will help us to serve in the kingdom of heaven. The parables of the Hidden Treasure and the Pearl of Great Price demand that we make our decision to gain the best of all treasures. This parable shows that the kingdom presents us with a standard for living and is therefore a testing ground for distinguishing between good and evil.

Background Information
This parable, as is true of all the others we have studied thus far, was delivered in Galilee. This one appears to have been given to the disciples privately, whereas the Parable of

the Sower, the Parable of the Tares, and the Parables of the Hidden Treasure and the Pearl of Great Price were all given to the large crowds that had gathered around the seashore to hear Jesus speak.

When many of us think of fishing, we associate it with a hobby, not as a way of livelihood. However, many of these people to whom Jesus was speaking looked at fishing as a way of life, their career. Fishing was, therefore, a very important activity. This parable must have caught the listening ear of the apostles, for several of them had been professional fishermen before beginning to follow Jesus. They knew the situation of which Jesus spoke.

Explaining the Text

A dragnet was a familiar scene around the Sea of Galilee. As the fishing boats went out each day for the "catch," they would be loaded with these nets. The net was such that it did not discriminate as to which fish were caught. Whatever came into the path of the great net were caught. Hence, fish of every kind would be netted.

There were different kinds of nets in the time of Jesus. At least three words used for "net" are well-known. First was the word δίκτυον (*diktuon*). This was a general word used for all nets, whether for fish or for fowl. Second was ἀμφίβλαστρον, *amphiblastron* (from ἀμφί, *amphi*, "around" and βάλλω, *ballo*, "to throw"). This was the word used for "the casting net." Third was the σαγήνη (*sagene*). This referred to the dragnet. It was a long net with the weighted part along the lower edge to cause it to drag along the lake bottom, with floats at the top. As the boat dragged it along, the net encircled the fish. Therefore, anything in the way of the net was caught. This explains the many kinds of fish that were caught on this occasion.

We saw earlier that this parable is considered by some writers to be closely related to the Parable of the Tares and they are therefore studied together. However, this parable differs from the Parable of the Tares in several ways. First, in "the Tares," the Devil is shown as sowing the seed as a deceiver. There is no such parallel in this parable. The different kinds of fish just happened to be in the way of the net. Second, in the Tares, or Weeds, the wheat and tares were closely similar and they were not separated because of their close similarity. In this parable, it was quite easy for these experienced fishermen to tell the difference between the various kinds of fish. Third, in the Tares, Jesus told the disciples to let both the wheat and tares grow together until the harvest. In this parable, the separation took place immediately after they were caught.

Purpose and Application

In some senses, this parable could be regarded as an eschatological (referring to the end of things) parable, for Jesus is showing how the fish will be separated as we will be separated when Jesus comes again. But perhaps in another sense, Jesus is saying that we can also make some decisions in this life concerning the association we have with those who are evil. There are three major concepts involved with the overall purpose of this parable.

First, *the church is composed of all kinds of people.* This is illustrated by the many kinds of fish that were caught in the dragnet. One of the most beautiful aspects of the kingdom of heaven is the fact that it is open to all people regardless of race, sex, social standing, or educational stature. All people are welcome! C.H. Dodd alludes to this heterogenous make-up of mankind.

Now the point of the story [the Parable of the Dragnet] is that when you are fishing with a dragnet you cannot expect to select your fish: your catch will be a mixed one: "all fish that come to your net," as our proverb has it. Similarly, the fishers of men must be prepared to cast their net widely over the whole field of human society. We are then reminded of the parable of the Great Feast, in which the invitation is given to all chance passers-by in highways and lanes. The mission of Jesus and His disciples involves an undiscriminating appeal to men of every class and type.[3]

This same thought is expressed by Buttrick when he wrote,

The net is flung on a wide sea without regard to creed, cast or clime: "God is no respecter of persons; but in every nation he that feareth him, and worketh righteousness, is accepted with him." None can escape those meshes, and the line of separation drawn across the "catch" over-passes all other lines.[4]

So, in our own time, the church is made up of different people. Each person has to be dealt with as a unique individual. We ought to treat people gently and with the greatest sense of love.

Second, *there will be a final judgment of all humankind.* Many in our day try to ignore the reality and certainty of a day of judgment. But Scripture is clear and forceful that there *will* be a final judgment (see Matt. 25:31–46; Heb. 9:27). This judgment will call all of us to account for the deeds we have done. As all of the fish were not palatable to the fisherman, so all who live according to the "flesh," or lower nature, are not palatable to Almighty God. It should be evident to the casual observer that our world is filled with wickedness. How can one look at the hideous crimes that are being committed and then not believe that eventually the criminals must pay for their crimes — if not in this world, certainly in the one to come.

Third, *there will be a final and irrevocable separation of the good from the evil.* In this life, we must coexist in the presence of evil. This not only helps strengthen us to be able to overcome temptation, it also shows the contrast between good and evil. In Matt. 25:31–46, Jesus clearly explains that there will be a separation. The righteous (who have been made righteous by the cross) will go to the right, the wicked will be on the left. Those on the right will be ushered into eternal life with God. The story of the Rich Man and Lazarus shows that this separation is irrevocable. There is no place in God's scheme of redemption for any type of universalism. Once this life is completed, there is no opportunity for a second chance. The righteous *will* be separated from the wicked, just as the bad fish will be separated from the good ones.

"Learning to Live" from this Parable

R.C. Trench makes an interesting observation concerning this parable. In comparing the Parable of the Tares and the Parable of the Dragnet, he wrote that "the central truth of that [Tares] is the *present* intermixture of the good and bad; of this [Dragnet], the *future* separation; of that [Tares], that men are not to effect the separation; of this [Dragnet], that the separation will one day be effected by God."[5] This is indeed a very important parable and has many applications to our everyday lives.

We should not despair; where there is good, evil tries to enter in. Satan does not become concerned when things are not going well. But when a church, a family, or an individual child of God begins to serve God, Satan is ready to pounce upon that situation. The Devil is not worried when things are not going well. He delights in confusion, disruption, and dissatisfaction in one's life; he does not need to be as actively involved in that kind of life as he does when things are going well. Show me a church that is doing God's will and I'll show you a church that must be on guard: Satan is on his way! So, we should not become discouraged when good is taking place and we find that evil is lurking around the corner.

It is alright for us to be sad when separations take place. The reason why we weep at the death of a loved one is the separation. Often we are well aware that death is a blessing, yet we mourn that death. Often we are not mourning the *death* of the person, but we are mourning the separation that has transpired. There will be a great separation when God judges the world; but when that happens, God's goodness will bring understanding to those who have come to know and love Him. When God selects the acceptable "fish" from the great catch of The Fisherman, those who are kept will be reserved for a marvelous and wonderful life to last an eternity.

We will never be able to entirely rid the church of evil in this world. Sin is always lurking at the door. Christians have often left a terrible misunderstanding in the minds of people in the world. We often act as if there is no sin in the church, or somehow give that impression. The world sees some Christians acting "holier than thou," or perhaps that is the mistaken perception. But sin *is* in the church; it will be present as long as humanity makes up the church. Those who assume the role of exhorter in the church should remember the statement by Paul, "Brothers, if someone is caught in a sin, you who are spiritual should restore him gently. But watch yourself, or you also may be tempted" (Gal. 6:1). Two great lessons can be seen here: First, because we ourselves are sinful, we ought to *deal gently* with those who are caught in sin. Second, if we exhort someone, we should be careful lest we be tempted and become trapped as well. We must exercise tender love and care in dealing with a weaker brother or sister in the Lord.

The kingdom of God (the church) is pure and faultless. It is marred by the sinfulness of human beings. But the church as God conceives it is "without wrinkle or any other blemish, but holy and blameless" (Eph. 5:27). Nevertheless, the warts and disfigurements that exist in the blessed church of Jesus Christ are all removed by the blood of the cross. We are washed and sanctified through baptism into His name; we are cleansed by the sacrificial death of Jesus on the cross. In the final analysis, all wickedness and evil will be removed from the church and those who have lived faithfully will be forever in the presence of God.

Endnotes for Chapter 5

[1] Taylor, *The Parables of Our Saviour*, p. 38ff. It might be noted here that Taylor studies this parable alongside the Parable of the Hidden Treasure and the Parable of the Pearl of Great Price. Buttrick also studies them together. See Buttrick, *The Parables of Jesus*, pp. 27ff.

[2] George A. Buttrick, *The Parables of Jesus*, pp. 26ff.

[3] C.H. Dodd, *The Parables of the Kingdom* (New York: Charles Scribner's Sons, 1961), p. 151.

[4] Buttrick, *The Parables of Jesus*, p. 37.

[5] Richard Chenevix Trench, *Notes on the Parables of Our Lord*, Popular Edition (Grand Rapids: Baker, 1948), p. 51.

EXCUSE ME, PLEASE
6

The Parable of Excuses: Luke 14:15–24

When one of those at the table with him heard this, he said to Jesus, "Blessed is the man who will eat at the feast in the kingdom of God."

Jesus replied: "A certain man was preparing a great banquet and invited many guests. At the time of the banquet he sent his servant to tell those who had been invited, 'Come, for everything is now ready.'

"But they all alike began to make excuses. The first said, 'I have just bought a field, and I must go and see it. Please excuse me.'

"Another said, 'I have just bought five yoke of oxen, and I'm on my way to try them out. Please excuse me.'

"Still another said, 'I just got married, so I can't come.'

"The servant came back and reported this to his master. Then the owner of the house became angry and ordered his servant, 'Go out quickly into the streets and alleys of the town and bring in the poor, the crippled, the blind and the lame.'

"'Sir,' the servant said, 'what you ordered has been done, but there is still room.'

"Then the master told his servant, 'Go out to the roads and country lanes and make them come in, so that my house will be full. I tell you, not one of those men who were invited will get a taste of my banquet'" (Luke 14:15–24).

Often in the personal ministry of Jesus, we find Him associated with feasts. His first miracle took place at a wedding feast; Jesus regularly went to the religious feasts prescribed by the Law of Moses; and there are at least two other parables that center around feasts or weddings (*cf.* Luke 14:1–11;

Matt. 22:1–14). Our celebration in heaven at the end of our pilgrimage on earth is described as a great feast. So it is not strange that Jesus would use a feast to show the importance of responsibility in our lives.

This parable is certainly a commentary on all of our lives. How many times have you searched for an excuse to avoid some responsibility? Frequently, I have tried to avoid making some needed visit to someone by searching for an excuse. Moses tried to forsake his responsibility to God when he was called to lead the Israelites out of Egypt. He made one excuse after another: he was timid, he wasn't a good speaker, the people wouldn't believe him. But in each case God showed that his excuses were unacceptable. Are your excuses for avoiding your responsibility to God or to your fellow-human being as weak as were Moses' excuses? Study with me this great Parable of Excuses; see if you can see yourself somewhere in this picture.

Background Information

This parable is recorded only by Luke, who sets the scene this way: "One Sabbath, when Jesus went to eat in the house of a prominent Pharisee, he was being carefully watched" (Luke 14:1). This is a significant introduction. It was on this Sabbath that Jesus healed a man. The Jewish law, and the fourth commandment, prohibited working on the Sabbath, and Jesus was perceived by those watching Him to have worked on the Sabbath; however, "they remained silent" (vs. 4). Even the Law had stipulated that in cases of emergency, it was permissible to do what was necessary on the Sabbath.

Furthermore, Jesus was in the house of a prominent Pharisee. The Pharisees were a sect of the Jews — as were the Sadducees and Essenes. Specifically, the Pharisees were very strict adherents not only to the law of Moses, but also to a rather complicated set of traditions compiled by various rabbis and other interpreters of the law. Often, Jesus and the Pharisees clashed as they confronted one another on points of the law. On one occasion, Jesus said that the Pharisees sat in Moses' seat and that one should "do everything they tell you. But do not do what they do, for they do not practice what they preach" (Matt. 23:3). They were a formidable force that Jesus had to cope with during His personal ministry.

Jesus had just commended humility. He had witnessed people striving for places of honor at the dinner in the Pharisee's house. He told them that "everyone who exalts himself will be humbled, and he who humbles himself will be exalted" (Luke 14:11). Undoubtedly, it is in this context that this parable of the excuses is given. What an honor to be invited to the home of an important person to dine with him; and what an insult it would be not to respond favorably to this kind of an invitation.

Feasts were frequently referred to in the New Testament. Because of the great time span between Jesus' day and ours, we do not know all of the customs of His day. But it appears that, on this occasion, two invitations were issued. Lightfoot gives one explanation of this:

> ... in keeping with Oriental customs, a general announcement was sent out to inform everybody of the coming event. The date was specified, but the exact hour was not. On the stated day, when all the preparations had been made and everything was in order, the man sent out his servant to tell his invited friends that the hour had arrived for the supper.[1]

Ordinarily, the kind of feast referred to here would have been given by a person of means, a rich person. Likewise, the guests would probably have been from the same class of people. One of those sitting with Jesus at the banquet said to Him, "Blessed is the man who will eat at the feast in the kingdom of God" (Luke 14:15). It appears that this statement caused Jesus to offer the parable that follows. In this parable, Jesus breaks social custom. After telling that some of those who were invited "began to make excuses," Jesus said the host extended his invitation to "the unworthy." This would have been almost unheard of in Jesus' time.

Explaining the Text

We just noted that, according to Oriental customs, two announcements of a banquet or feast would be sent: the first one would have a date but not the time; the second would be sent out when the feast was about to be served. It was an honor for one to receive such an invitation, so it would be highly unlikely that the invitation would be cancelled and certainly not spurned. In this parable, we are introduced to several interesting textual items.

We are told that the recipients of the invitation "began to make excuses" (vs. 18). The Greek word for "to make excuse" is παραιτεῖσθαι (*paraiteisthai*), and it means to refuse, to beg off, or "consider me excused." The *Expositor's Greek Testament* observes that this was a polite way to ask to be excused. Perhaps there was no intention to insult or to spurn the invitation.

This was no ordinary meal; it was a great feast. Arndt and Gingrich[2] suggest that the two words δεῖπνον μέγα (*deipnon mega*, literally, "a great feast") actually refer to a formal dinner or banquet. One would assume that a person who could give such a banquet would be a person of unusual importance. This is certainly in keeping with the importance of the heavenly "feast" that all of us have been invited to attend.

"They all alike began to make excuses" (vs. 18). "All alike," from ἀπὸ μιᾶς (*apo mias*) may be more accurately translated, "at once." In other words, they gave no serious

```

thought to the invitation, but "began at once to make excuses." It does not appear that they had conspired together in their refusal to attend the feast. Their decisions were made quickly and decisively.

When those whom the host invited refused his invitation, he told his servants to "Go quickly into the streets and alleys (from πλατείας [*plateias*] or "street corners," and ῥύμας [*hrumas*], "alleys") of the town and bring in the poor, the crippled, the blind and the lame" (Luke 14:21,23). "Lanes," or "hedges" as some translate, comes from φραγμός (*phragmos*), and it refers to the hedges beside which the vagrants lie. In other words, he was offering his feast to the outcast. In fact, he told his servants to "make them come in" (vs. 23). The word ἀναγκάζω (*anagkazo*) carries a form of oriental courtesy in which a guest who has politely refused is urged to respond until he does so. So, the invitation was urgent.

## Purpose and Application

This parable has a very clear application, but there are also some underlying lessons which are just as important. It is evidently levelled at the Pharisees and others who were refusing to give Jesus an appropriate hearing. The Lord is telling them that God will certainly turn from those who were His chosen people to others (the Gentiles) to invite to His feast. People in the parable who had offered excuses fell into two categories: those involving earthly possessions (the man who had bought the field and the one who purchased the five yoke of oxen) and those involving earthly ties (the man who was just married). Although it was out of place, the man who married the wife was perhaps more justified than the others, for the law provided that a newly married man should dedicate the first year to his wife and was not eligible for military service during that year.
```

This parable, therefore, was spoken against the Jewish people, who had by and large, refused Jesus' offer of salvation. They could certainly offer ample excuses, but none of them was valid in view of the greatness of the feast. It was a *mega deipnon*, a great feast or banquet.

If the Chosen (the Jews) *refuse the invitation, then those whom they regarded as accursed* (the Gentiles) *will be invited.* After all the gospel is for all people. The only ones who will not reap the benefits of the gospel will be those who refuse to accept it. What one possesses does not determine his relationship with God, but what one *is* is significant. All are invited to the Great Feast, and the invitation is accepted by being receptive and obedient to the gift of the Master. As indicated earlier, this parable was likely spoken against the Jewish people of Jesus' day who had refused His offer of salvation. Paul would later "shake the dust off of his feet" regarding the Jews and turn to the Gentiles who were to receive the gospel (see Acts 18:6).

"Learning to Live" from this Parable

We are living in a world that offers a wide variety of alternatives. We often use these opportunities to avoid serving God. It is so easy for us to opt for the convenient or the pleasurable and to leave God out of our plans. In this parable, the three who offered excuses had other options than having to attend the banquet. They were good reasons within the right context; but their importance did not compare with the values inherent in serving God.

Not one of the excuses was sufficient for their refusal of such an important invitation. How can one compare the honor and pleasure of attending such an important banquet with going to approve a field or test oxen? Not even a recent marriage was a sufficient excuse. Jesus is very clear in demanding that He must have *first* place or *no* place in our lives (see Matt. 16:24ff). We often sing songs like "Jesus is All the World to Me," and yet we are unwilling to give Him that first place at times. This is certainly one of the important lessons from this parable.

Sometimes the most precious things in our lives are used as an excuse to neglect our proper relationship with God. I have actually known of parents who used their children as excuses for neglecting their duty to God. Certainly our children are important, but we must not use them as an excuse to allow us to avoid service to God. God is first!

God's grace is all-encompassing enough to reach anyone. When those who refused the invitation excluded themselves, the Host sent for those least likely to be invited to such a banquet. We must look in unlikely places for those to honor with an invitation to God's salvation. Not the high, not the mighty, not the honorable will necessarily be most willing to accept God; rather, those who are hurting, those who are needy, and those whose lives have no great goals are often more willing to accept the Lord. We must go after God's people wherever they may be found.

If we do not want to serve God, we can always find a reason (or excuse) not to follow Him. We are good at rationalizing our behavior. I suggest we go to God's word as though it were the first time we have ever read it and ask, "What will you have me do?" This kind of obedience will be pleasing to the Master.

Endnotes for Chapter 6

[1] Neil R. Lightfoot, *Lessons from the Parables* (Grand Rapids: Baker, 1965), p. 101.

[2] William F. Arndt and F. Wilbur Gingrich, *A Greek-English Lexicon of the New Testament and Other Early Christian Literature* (Chicago: The University of Chicago Press, 1979), p. 173.

CONCLUSION TO PART I: LIFE IN THE KINGDOM

Nothing is so vast and nothing is so all-encompassing as the kingdom of God, or the kingdom of heaven. It literally fills the world and it includes everyone who has truly placed his/her life under God's control. It includes, but is not confined to, the church for which Jesus gave His life.

This first part of our study has examined the relationship, or role, of the kingdom in our personal lives. The kingdom should not be conceived as some nebulous entity that is hard for us to identify. The kingdom of God resides within those who have been born again through baptism into Christ (John 3:1–8), who have allowed God and His kingdom into their lives (Luke 17:20–21), and who have allowed King Jesus to rule over them.

As seed, the kingdom becomes a part of our lives through the germination of the seed of the kingdom (the revealed word of God), the natural growth processes of that seed, and an attempt to keep what is foreign to the kingdom out of our lives. We have seen that Satan is constantly on the prowl and will do whatever is in his power to destroy us and kingdom-living within us.

The kingdom is truly a valuable possession. Embracing and cherishing the kingdom is worth all of life's possessions. In a real sense, only those who have experienced the kingdom can truly feel the worth of the kingdom. Jesus declared that our primary goal is to "seek first" God's kingdom and His righteousness, and then life takes on its real focus (see Matt. 6:33).

The kingdom was the focal point of Israelite theology and it is central to all that Jesus is to us. John the Baptist came preaching the kingdom, and Jesus came preaching the kingdom. Our goal is to appropriate the kingdom to our lives in order to experience the greatness of our fellowship with God and with His Son, the Christ.

PART II: DISCIPLESHIP PARABLES

A disciple is a learner. The last three years of Jesus' life on earth were spent training those who would take His kingdom message to all the world. In fact, some of Jesus' parting words to His disciples were, "All authority in heaven and on earth has been given to me. Therefore go and make disciples of all nations, . . ." (Matt. 28:18–19). Discipleship, therefore, demands that we "make disciples" of all peoples.

Since Jesus was guiding His disciples to be better teachers, His disciples were learning from the Master Teacher how to administer the kingdom to all people. One of the most frequently used words for disciple is μαθητής (*mathetes*), which means "pupil, apprentice, disciple, adherent."[1]

Discipleship means putting Christ first in one's life. Jesus is never satisfied being in second place. He either wants *first place*, or no place (cf. Matt. 16:24–25). Jesus taught that the kingdom of God also demands first place: "But seek first his kingdom and his righteousness. . . ." (Matt. 6:33). Discipleship was a supreme sacrifice for those who followed Jesus.

In this second division of our study, we look at discipleship as portrayed in the parables. We shall also be looking at discipleship as more than just the process of learning. We shall be looking at some of the specific attitudes which should characterize disciples: sharing, hospitality, humility, forgiveness, love, patience, and other like attitudes. Discipleship involves behavior. Disciples *follow* their master. The attitudes which characterize disciples will produce unique types of behavioral characteristics in the lives of those seeking to be disciples. Hence, we shall be looking at some parables which emphasize such behavioral characteristics as were mentioned above. When these behavioral traits are seen in our lives, then our attitudes will be influences in a very positive way. Those who are learning to live for Jesus will find that these parables will become a source of solace and encouragement.

Earlier we noted that the parables are a rich storehouse of truths which can provide a resource for us when we are discouraged or despairing. Study these parables in order to provide a bridge between your ailing, sin-sick soul and the Great Physician, Who can provide every need you may have.

Endnotes to Part II Introduction

[1] Arndt & Gingrich, *A Greek-English Lexicon*, p. 485.

WHO IS MY NEIGHBOR?
7

The Parable of the Good Samaritan: Luke 10:25–37

On one occasion an expert in the law stood up to test Jesus. "Teacher," he asked, "what must I do to inherit eternal life?"

"What is written in the Law?" he replied. "How do you read it?"

He answered: "'Love the Lord your God with all your heart and with all your soul and with all your strength and with all your mind'; and, 'Love your neighbor as yourself.'"

"You have answered correctly," Jesus replied. "Do this and you will live."

But he wanted to justify himself, so he asked Jesus, "And who is my neighbor?"

In reply Jesus said: "A man was going down from Jerusalem to Jericho, when he fell into the hands of robbers. They stripped him of his clothes, beat him and went away, leaving him half dead. A priest happened to be going down the same road, and when he saw the man, he passed by on the other side. So too, a Levite, when he came to the place and saw him, passed by on the other side. But a Samaritan, as he traveled, came where the man was; and when he saw him, he took pity on him. He went to him and bandaged his wounds, pouring on oil and wine. Then he put the man on his own donkey, took him to an inn and took care of him. The next day he took out two silver coins and gave them to the innkeeper. 'Look after him,' he said, 'and when I return, I will reimburse you for any extra expense you may have.'

"Which of these three do you think was a neighbor to the man who fell into the hands of robbers?"

The expert in the law replied, "The one who had mercy on him."

Jesus told him, "Go and do likewise" (Luke 10:25–37).

David Wenham recently wrote a book in which he

presents the parables as "Pictures of Revolution."[1] Two penetrating comments that he makes are very fitting here. "Jesus'
call to love the Samaritan and the enemy was indeed revolutionary in the context of his day."[2] Later, we will notice why
this was a "revolutionary" teaching here. The other comment:
"The revolution of God means the bringing back of all God's
world into peace. The parable of the good Samaritan is the
imperative of this revolution."[3] Perhaps our world has never
been without a significant amount of racial/cultural/ethnic
prejudice, not to mention religious prejudice.

Although this parable has much more significance than
just its teaching on the equality of human beings, it certainly
does emphasize how important the individual is, regardless of
what he/she looks like or how he/she thinks. James Montgomery Boice states that

> ... in some ways the parable of the Good Samaritan is the most
> straightforward of all the Lord's stories. It is clarity itself — the
> story of a Samaritan who showed mercy to the victim of a beating
> and robbery, and who thus acted as a "neighbor" toward him. We
> are to "do likewise." Yet the story is one of the hardest of the
> Lord's parables to expound.[4]

This is one of the most well-known parables that Jesus
spoke. Luke spoke frequently of the humanitarian work of
Jesus' life. Is it significant that Luke, a physician, would be
interested in the poor and the downtrodden? This parable
should touch the strings of the hearts of both those who are
able to help others as well as those needing help.

Background Information

This parable is almost universally referred to as "The
Parable of the Good Samaritan." Recently, someone remarked
that the expression "good Samaritan" in Jesus' day would be
a marvelous example of an "oxymoron," that is, the combina-

tion of two conflicting terms. However, it is interesting to note that nowhere is the word "Good" used to describe this man. He was a Samaritan whose deeds of mercy and kindness "bought" for him this title. The fact that he was a *Samaritan*, nevertheless, is significant. Following the Babylonian Captivity in the 6th century B.C., many of the people who were not desirable to the Babylonians were left in the land of Canaan. They intermarried with the people of the land (becoming "half-breeds," according to the Israelites) and were unacceptable to the more rigid Israelites. They still held to the Pentateuch (first five books of the Old Testament) and still continued to worship the God of the Bible.

Yet through the years, there was a built-in resentment between the Israelites after their return from captivity and the Samaritans who had remained in the land. Jewish people of Jesus' day looked on the Samaritans as though they were "dogs." So, for Jesus to use the Samaritan as the "good" man of the parable must have great significance. From the text, we conclude that the man who was mistreated was a Jewish man, though the text does not say.

We do not know when or on what occasion this parable was given, although we do know it was given in response to the lawyer's question of "Who is my neighbor?" Luke simply says "On one occasion an expert in the law stood up to test Jesus" (Luke 10:25). This man who questioned Jesus was an "expert in the law" (νομικός, *nomikos*, "learned in the law").[5] He was an expert in the Law of Moses. Although he was putting Jesus to the test, there is nothing to suggest that he was being malicious in his intent; however, many Jewish leaders in similar situations during Jesus' ministry had done so out of malicious intentions. Taylor has this observation,

> But two things must strike every attentive reader. The first is, that
> the parable was not so much an answer to the question formally

put by the lawyer, as an exposure of the state of heart which the putting of that question revealed. . . . But the second peculiarity of this parable is, that it is not an allegory, each figure in which represents a spiritual analogue; but simply an illustrative example of the working of benevolence, as contrasted with that of selfishness.[6]

Explaining the Text

The area where Jesus placed the setting of this parable is a well-known one. Wenham gives this brief, yet accurate, description of the geographical setting:

In his parable Jesus describes a man going down the road from Jerusalem to Jericho. Today there is a fine modern road sweeping down from the hills of Jerusalem into the great Rift Valley, where Jericho is situated. But when reading Jesus' parable we have to remember that the roads in Jesus' Palestine were very rudimentary and rough — the famous Roman road system had not yet been extended to Palestine — and that travel on foot was slow and also dangerous, because of brigands. It was desirable and common to travel in groups. The Jerusalem to Jericho road, although it was quite a busy route, was particularly hazardous. In about seventeen miles it descended steeply (from a height of 2,500 feet above sea-level to 770 feet below) through desolate and craggy limestone hills — ideal terrain for bandits. Jesus' hearers will have been familiar with the scene, and the description of the man being set upon, brutally beaten and left half-dead will have made uncomfortable sense.[7]

"Down" from Jerusalem was not only a familiar phrase, but it was also an accurate one, for in whatever direction one went from Jerusalem, it was "down." Jerusalem was situated on the top of several hills, or "mounts."

There are several words in this parable that would be interesting to study; however, only two will be included here. One word we will look at is at the very center of the parable: the word *neighbor*. Literally, from the Old English, it means "one near," and our word is an adaptation of the Old English word "nigh-bor." The Greek word here is πλήσιον (*plesion*), and its basic meaning is "one who is nearby." But, the Gospels give it a much broader meaning, including the whole brotherhood of mankind (see Matt. 5:43ff.). So, our neighbor is one to whom we can do good.

The second word is δικαιῶσαι (*dikaiosai*). It is a form of the word "righteous," but here it means to make a person righteous, or more correctly to help one "to keep his character" as a righteous person. Undoubtedly, this lawyer saw himself as a good person. He was a lover and interpreter of the law, and when he asked Jesus who his neighbor was, he "wanted to justify himself" (see Luke 10:29). Most of us like to look at our lives with an end to "justify" our behavior. We tend to rationalize our actions. This man appears to be rationalizing his actions in his own mind, because he saw himself as righteous.

Purpose and Application

The primary purpose of this parable is seen in Jesus' answer to the lawyer's question. Jesus wanted us to know about the universality of His message and kingdom. We have a responsibility toward every person in the world, regardless of race, sex, culture, religion. We have the responsibility of "being a neighbor" to them. This parable suggests at least two great lessons for us.

Religion is much more than worship. All too often, we allow our religious lives to be stifled by ritualism. The priest and the Levite may have been on their way to or from the temple where they served God in a very unique way. But Jesus is saying to us that sometimes our "acts" of worship or our ritual must give way to the "here-and-now" demands we face. *The major difference between the Samaritan and the priest and Levite is that the Samaritan had a compassionate heart.* Don't misunderstand! Surely the priest and Levite were caring people. Their whole lives were wrapped up in serving God. But we must put our service to God in the right focus. Sometimes it may be more important for us to act like a good neighbor even if it demands that we have to postpone some ritual or some practice of formal worship. We must have the wisdom to tell the difference rather than use the "neighborliness" as an excuse for *not* fulfilling our responsibilities to God. It is possible for a Christian whose total life is involved in serving God to make inappropriate choices in what is most important.

Compassion can truly be seen only through the character of one's actions. Love is an invisible thing. You cannot draw a picture of "love"; you cannot describe its dimensions nor tell its color. The only way we can demonstrate love is through our actions. Jesus made this such a high priority for our lives that He said, "All men will know that you are my disciples if you love one another" (John 13:35). The Samaritan truly demonstrated Jesus' lesson in this parable through his total and unconditional love for the stranger. No matter that the wounded man may have acted unwisely in going where he should not have gone alone (on the dangerous Jericho road). No matter that the wounded man was one of those who hated the Samaritans. He was in need, and the Samaritan responded! Christianity can really be seen when our actions cross over the boundaries of race, culture, class, or economic standards.

"Learning to Live" from this Parable

Through the years, I have found this parable to be particularly helpful to me. Somewhere, I do not know where, I came across three sets of lessons that can be learned from this parable. I submit them with apologies to whoever wrote them

WHO IS MY NEIGHBOR?

with regrets for not being able to give credit for the statements.

Three rules of life are illustrated by this parable. *The Iron Rule* is illustrated by the robber who mistreated and robbed the man. He was ruled by the philosophy that "might makes right." This rule is still followed by many in our world. Just because one is a bigger or stronger or has an advantage over someone else, does not give that person the right to mistreat others. *The Silver Rule* is illustrated by the priest and the Levite. They did nothing either destructive nor constructive. They were ruled by the philosophy of "tending to self and leaving others alone." They actually did nothing at all. *The Golden Rule* is illustrated by the Good Samaritan. His philosophy was "Do unto others as you would have them do unto you." He was willing to take the risk and help the other person.

Three attitudes of life are shown by this parable. *The Politician's Attitude* (and no offense is intended to all those honest and dedicated politicians) is described by the question, "What can I get out of it?" Or, "what's in it for me?" *The Shirker's Attitude* approaches life with the attitude, "How can I get out of it?" All too often, many Christians approach service to God with that kind of an attitude. It is not enough to do just what I *have to do*. I must be willing to go "the extra mile." *The Christian's Attitude* is characterized by the question, "What more can I do?" This is the essence of that greatest of all love, *agape*. *Agape*, ἀγάπη, is a non-self-centered behavior. It is concerned for the welfare of others.

Three philosophies of life are illustrated in the following ways: The philosophy of life of the self-centered person, illustrated by the robber, was "What is thine is mine; I'll take it." The philosophy of the miser, illustrated by the priest and Levite, was "What is mine is mine; I'll keep it." The philosophy of life of the Christian, demonstrated by the Samaritan, is "What is mine is thine; you can have it if you need it more than I do." Each of us has to choose, in so many situations of life, which of these philosophies we will practice.

William Barclay provides a very fitting conclusion to this chapter. In answer to the question, "Who is my neighbor," Barclay says that "Jesus' answer involves three things.

(i) "We must help a man even when he has brought his trouble on himself, as the traveller had done.

(ii) "Any man of any nation who is in need is our neighbour. Our help must be as wide as the love of God.

(iii) "The help must be practical and not consist merely in *feeling* sorry. No doubt the priest and the Levite felt a pang of pity for the wounded man, but they *did* nothing. Compassion, to be real, must issue in deeds."[8]

Endnotes for Chapter 7

[1] David Wenham, *The Parables of Jesus: Pictures of Revolution* (London: Hodder & Stoughton, 1989).

[2] *Ibid.*, p. 159.

[3] *Ibid.*, p. 161.

[4] James Montgomery Boice, *The Parables of Jesus* (Chicago: Moody Press, 1983), p. 148.

[5] Arndt & Gingrich, *A Greek-English Lexicon*, p. 541.

[6] Taylor, *The Parables of Our Saviour*, pp. 227–228.

[7] Wenham, *The Parables of Jesus*, p. 155.

[8] William Barclay, *The Gospel of Luke*, Revised Edition (Philadelphia: Westminster, 1975), pp. 140–141.

THE WAY UP IS DOWN
8

The Parable of Seats at a Feast: Luke 14:1–14

One Sabbath, when Jesus went to eat in the house of a prominent Pharisee, he was being carefully watched. There in front of him was a man suffering from dropsy. Jesus asked the Pharisees and experts in the law, "Is it lawful to heal a man on the Sabbath or not?" But they remained silent. So taking hold of the man, he healed him and sent him away.

Then he asked them, "If one of you has a son or an ox that falls into a well on the Sabbath day, will you not immediately pull him out?" And they had nothing to say.

When he noticed how the guests picked the places of honor at the table, he told them this parable: "When someone invites you to a wedding feast, do not take the place of honor, for a person more distinguished than you may have been invited. If so, the host who invited both of you will come and say to you, 'Give this man your seat.' Then, humiliated, you will have to take the least important place. But when you are invited, take the lowest place, so that when your host comes, he will say to you, 'Friend, move up to a better place.' Then you will be honored in the presence of all your guests. For everyone who exalts himself will be humbled, and he who humbles himself will be exalted."

Then Jesus said to his host, "When you give a luncheon or dinner, do not invite your friends, your brothers or relatives, or your rich neighbors; if you do, they may invite you back and so you will be repaid. But when you give a banquet, invite the poor, the crippled, the lame, the blind, and you will be blessed. Although they cannot repay you, you will be repaid at the resurrection of the righteous" (Luke 14:1–14).

In a previous chapter, we noted that Jesus is regarded by some people as a revolutionary. In fact, we saw that a recent author on the parables sees the parables as "pictures of revolution."[1] Whether you accept this claim by Wenham or not, it is certainly clear that much of Jesus' life was "lived on the edge." He was constantly under close scrutiny and frequently the object of criticism by the leaders of his day. In the next section of this chapter, we note some of the circumstances that caused Jesus to be specially watched at this time in His ministry.

Background Information

On the occasion of this parable, Jesus was "being carefully watched" (Luke 14:1). One incident that influenced the giving of this parable was the fact that He had just performed a great humanitarian miracle: he had healed "a man suffering from dropsy" (from ὑδρωπικός, *hudropikos*). Dropsy was a disease that, in Palestine, showed itself in two different but related forms: either the disease attacked the limbs and the body so that they were distended with water (hence, the first part of the word ὑδρω-, [*hudro-*] from a word meaning "water") *or* the disease was confined to the lower body which caused liver problems.[2] Why the afflicted man would be at this dinner, we do not know unless someone had brought him there to be healed by Jesus. Regardless of the reason, this healing caused the consternation of the guests in the Pharisee's house.

Jesus knew their minds; He knew that they were watching to see what He would do. This caused Him to ask the Pharisees and experts in the law, "Is it lawful to heal on the Sabbath or not?" Luke says that "they remained silent" (Luke 14:3–4), so Jesus healed the man and sent him away. We can imagine the tremendous feelings of resentment against Jesus that these guests held. Jesus then asked them, "If one of you has a son [see next section for a discussion on whether this is "son" or "donkey"] or an ox that falls into a well on the Sabbath day, will you not immediately pull him out?" (verse 5) And they did not answer Him. We can almost feel the tension that grew in the room, but no one dared attack Jesus. Many people are constantly watching for reasons to criticize others' actions, especially when those actions run counter to what they may *believe* is right.

A second incident which provoked this parable was Jesus' observance of "how the guests picked the places of honor at the table" as they began to be seated. In those days, the customs for eating included a table that would be set in a "U" shape. The table was usually low, perhaps a foot and a half from the floor. Those dining would lie on pillows on the floor with their feet pointing away from the table, leaning on their left arm to eat. The host would usually sit at the "head" or at the crux of the "U" of the table. Honored guests were normally seated at the "head" of the table. As guests would arrive, they would often try to be seated as near the host as possible. Since time was not as important a factor in their culture as in ours, guests would be arriving at different times because the exact hour of the feast would not usually be announced. It was in this situation that Jesus was observing how the guests chose where they would sit. This provided an excellent background for Him to teach a lesson on humility.

Explaining the Text

A little earlier, it was mentioned that there is some confusion over whether Jesus used the word "son" or "donkey." There are variations in some of the manuscripts. Various manuscripts have the Greek word υἱός (*huios*) which means "son" and others have ὄνος (*onos*) which means "a donkey or an ass." For the lesson that Jesus is teaching, it makes no difference to the intended meaning. In either case, the law of Moses provided for taking care of emergencies on the Sabbath day. In fact, the matter of what is lawful on the Sabbath is not actually a part of this parable; it is only a part of the context which provided Jesus with a point of reference to teach them.

When Jesus had "cornered" the Pharisees and experts in the law, Luke states that "They had nothing to say" (vs. 6). Literally, this statement means, "They could not answer." Jesus' argument was too forceful for them. If they tenaciously held that absolutely nothing may be done on the Sabbath day, they would be made to look like they believed that their ox and donkey (or son) was more important than the healing of a human being (or just *any* human being if the word here is "son"). So, they were placed in a real dilemma.

One other interesting statement needs a word of explanation. Jesus said that if one takes a lower seat when he deserves a more honorable one, the host will say "Friend, move up to a better place" or literally "come up higher" (from προσανάβηθι, *prosanabethi*). It literally means to go *up* to the higher position offered by the host.

Purpose and Application

Jesus appears to be addressing two audiences: the host of the dinner and those who picked the places of honor. In this passage, the last part about those who ought to be invited to such a dinner almost sounds like an afterthought. However, the paragraph has a very close relationship to the whole theme. Jesus may have noticed that the host had invited only those who were people of honor or importance to the host. None was there who was needy or to whom this invitation would be an unusually great honor. So, Jesus addressed this portion of the parabolic teaching to the host. We need to learn the great lesson of hospitality from this. Certainly we are not wrong to invite those we know and love. But Jesus is teaching that this should not be the sole focus of our hospitality. We should reach out to those less fortunate than we are. Isn't it significant that a central factor of Jesus' focus was on the poor, the maimed, the blind and the crippled? Surely there is a impelling motivation to us today to be more concerned about the needs of others rather than always concentrating on our own desires.

Jesus is teaching that *the only way UP in God's kingdom is to go down.* Choose the lowly seats and you may be asked to move up to a more honorable place, Jesus said. To use a term a good friend of mine uses, *we should be people of the towel* (see John 13:1–17). It is necessary for us to become servants in order to gain the Lord's attention. Jesus was prophesied to be the suffering servant. He came not to be ministered to, but to minister to others. "No servant is greater than his master, nor is a messenger greater than the one who sent him" (John 13:16).

To be exalted, one needs to be humbled. Dr. E.W. McMillan used to say, "Humiliation always precedes exaltation." Long ago, I heard the statement, "No man can lift himself by his own bootstraps." We cannot be great by extolling our own virtues. James very appropriately summarized the Christian's attitude toward self as follows: "Humble yourselves before the Lord, and he will lift you up" (James 4:10). And Peter wrote, ". . . Clothe yourselves with humility toward one another, because 'God opposes the proud but gives grace to the humble.' Humble yourselves, therefore, under God's mighty hand, that he may lift you up in due time" (1 Pet. 5:5–6; see also Phil. 2:3–4).

"Learning to Live" from this Parable

When I compare myself with Christ, I see my terrible wretched nature. It is indeed a very humbling experience. We are told our "attitude should be the same as that of Christ Jesus" (Phil. 2:5). The Son of God forsook all that He had, became a servant of humankind, and died the most humiliating death one could experience — *all for me!* He was not concerned during His life on earth with how important He was. Christ Jesus did not look for the honorable seats in any of His relationships. He was a "man of the towel"; He gave all, that He might redeem all.

We should be greatly humbled when we look at the self-sacrificing Savior, than at ourselves! Even the strongest person among us is woefully weak — physically and spiritually. We are a people who have turned our eyes and our ears away from God. We are mired in moral weakness and failure. There is no way out except through the cross of Christ. The moral weakness and failures of humanity should humble us; yet, thank God, through the blood of Christ we can feel strong. Not because we have any strength; but, because Christ makes us strong and elevates us to the highest position. Our faith and obedience to Christ puts us into covenant relationship with Him, and we receive grace which is provided by Christ.

We should never do good with the idea, "What can I get in return?" This is illustrated by Jesus' remarks to the host after He spoke the parable. When we give a luncheon or dinner, Jesus says, do not invite those who are closest to us; rather, "invite the poor, the crippled, the lame, the blind" (Luke 14:12–14). This is the only way that we can truly be assured of being repaid, and Jesus told us that the repayment will be "at the judgment of the righteous" (cf. verse 14). After all, what we can do for our fellow-pilgrims in this brief earthly journey is far more important than all the possessions we can amass or all of the great reputations we can gain for ourselves. The real way to find the highest place in the kingdom is to kneel down before the throne of God and offer our lives as living sacrifices.

Just as the Jewish people became entangled in their legalism, so our traditions and personal opinions often get in the way of our service to God. By healing the man with dropsy, Jesus challenged the Jewish leaders to reconsider their traditions regarding the Sabbath laws. In the same way, He challenges us to leave our traditional way of doing things and, instead, work for the salvation of men and women. Sometimes the greatest service to Christ can be performed "on the way to church" rather than in the assembly. Don't misunderstand! The church is important — Christ died for it! But the church is a "hospital" for sin-infected humanity. Let us rise to the challenge and reach out with the healing touch of Christ.

Endnotes for Chapter 8

[1] David Wenham, *The Parables of Jesus.*

[2] See "Dropsy" in *The International Standard Bible Encyclopedia*, ed., James Orr (Grand Rapids: Eerdmans, 1955), Vol. II, p. 880.

PATIENT PERSISTENCE PAYS
9

The Parable of the Persistent Widow: Luke 18:1-8

Then Jesus told his disciples a parable to show them that they should always pray and not give up. He said: "In a certain town, there was a judge who neither feared God nor cared about men. And there was a widow in that town who kept coming to him with the plea, 'Grant me justice against my adversary.'

"For some time he refused. But finally he said to himself, 'Even though I don't fear God or care about men, yet because this widow keeps bothering me, I will see that she gets justice, so that she won't eventually wear me out with her coming!'"

And the Lord said, "Listen to what the unjust judge says. And will not God bring about justice for his chosen ones, who cry out to him day and night? Will he keep putting them off? I tell you, he will see that they get justice, and quickly. However, when the Son of Man comes, will he find faith on the earth?" (Luke 18:1-8).

The Parable of the Persistent Widow is difficult for many to understand. Some conclude that God may lose His patience with us if we "nag" him to answer our prayers. As we shall see, this is not the lesson that Jesus wanted us to receive from the parable. On the other hand, we do learn that God "is not slow in keeping his promise, as some understand slowness. He is patient with you, not wanting anyone to perish, but everyone to come to repentance" (2 Pet. 3:9-10).

Background Information

In the verses immediately preceding this parable and the

one following it, Jesus had been addressing a very important topic: the coming of the kingdom. The Pharisees had asked Him when the kingdom of God would come (Luke 17:20). Jesus replied that the kingdom would not be the kind of kingdom that men think of most frequently. Rather, it would be a kingdom within the spiritual center of each believer. The coming of the kingdom in its fullness would usher in the eternal reign of God in the hearts of human beings. Next, Jesus gave some illustrations to show that the coming of the kingdom would be unexpected, and the redeemed ones would be those who are willing to lose their lives in order to preserve them.

The nature of the kingdom of God is certainly not like the kingdoms of the world. In worldly kingdoms, there is a striving after power, position and prestige. Jesus impresses us through this parable that the inner person of the redeemed is far from being a power/position-seeking individual. Rather, those who are able to humble themselves and persistently serve the Master are the ones who would be saved.

The centrality of the kingdom to the parable would almost cause one to include this with the "kingdom parables" already studied. However, it is included here because it deals more specifically with the theme of discipleship than it does specifically with the theme of kingdom. Here, attitudes which are consonant with discipleship are demonstrated: humility, persistence, and a dedicated resolve to cling to God.

It is easy for the Christian to give up on God, because God does not use a calendar like we do to determine when He causes things to happen. We are so time-bound that we live expectantly, but we rely on clocks, times and seasons. God does not do that. With God, "a day is like a thousand years, and a thousand years are like a day" (2 Pet. 3:9). Don't give up on God. Understanding this, we should not conclude that

God loses His patience with us and only answers our prayers to keep us from pestering Him.

The parable does emphasize the need for us to be persistent, for God wants to see that we really depend on Him for all we have. The setting of this parable is probably that of a Roman judge and a Jewish woman, because one judge did not constitute a Jewish court. "According to Pharisaical traditions, Jewish persons were forbidden to go to non-Jewish courts. Paul indicates that in the early church this same rule should be followed (1 Cor. 5:12–6:8). People often went to a Gentile judge 'if thereby, appealing to some political or fiscal argument, they could have their opponent's rights frustrated or could force him to do what the customary law would have left alone. [Derrett, "Law in the New Testament," p. 184.']"[1]

A widow's life in Israel was a difficult one. When her husband died, she lost many of her personal rights. She had no one to plead her case. It is likely that she would have children, for Jewish girls often were married in their early teens, bore children, and hence had no independence of their own. The widow in this parable likely had no money, could not appeal to someone as an advocate; hence, her only weapon was to "worry the judge" until he decided in her favor. Letting her continue to "badger" him, the judge's reputation could be greatly damaged (see the comments in the next section). In other words, the judge probably was not concerned with the woman's needs as much as he was concerned about his own reputation as a judge.

This parable is found only in the gospel written by Luke. As we shall see later on, the parable does give us an interesting portrait of God. He is not a retributive God who wants to make us grovel at His feet before He will answer our prayers. Instead, He is a wise and loving God who will answer our prayers. He does not answer them according to our "timetable;" rather, He answers them when the right time comes.

Explaining the Text

This parable poses some problems for some interpreters. First, if taken literally throughout, it places God in a rather untenable position: He is the God of patience (see 2 Pet. 3:9), yet He becomes impatient with those who continually call upon Him, if He is likened to the unjust judge. But rather than comparing God to the judge, Jesus contrasts the unjust judge with the totally just and righteous God. The same Greek word, μακροθυμέω (*makrothumeo*, "to have patience, be forbearing"), is used in both of these verses (Luke 18:7 and 2 Pet. 3:9). Jesus said, "Will he *keep putting them off?*" or, "and yet he is longsuffering over them" (American Standard Version). Contrast that with the judge who did not accommodate the widow because he was patient or forbearing, but rather in order to stop her from pestering him.

Second, if the total text is taken literally, it sounds as though the widow and the judge may have "come to blows" in their confrontations. The expression "that she won't *eventually wear me out* (emphasis mine) with her coming" is a translation of ὑπωπιάζη με (*hupopiadze me*, literally meaning "to strike under the eye, give a black eye").[2] Now, it does not fit in with the context that any physical confrontation took place. In fact, it would be most unlikely for a widow to actually strike the judge or give him a black eye. This reference is actually referring to the reputation that the judge fears if he does not rule in her behalf — even though he does not fear God or man. So, the judge answered her request because of his own reputation.

Third, the woman was persistent. She did not give up; so, Jesus spoke the parable "to show them that they should always pray and not give up." The expression "not give up" comes from ἐγκακεῖν (*egkakein*, literally, "not to give in to evil, to turn coward, lose heart, behave badly"). She persisted until her prayer was answered.

Purpose and Application

This parable teaches us the power and preciousness of prayer. Until we can learn to humble ourselves, we cannot offer an effectual prayer. Wenham wrote,

> Prayer is an expression of human weakness, but also a weapon of divine power. The thought of God's power being displayed in and through human weakness is an important theme in Paul's letters (e.g. 2 Cor. 12:9–10): prayer is the expression of our powerlessness and of our dependence on God, and at the same time the most powerful means we have of collaborating in God's work.[3]

This parable provides us a powerful lesson on prayer.

We ought always to pray and not to give up. Luke states that this was the purpose of the parable: ". . . to show them that they should always pray and not give up." There are so many statements in Scripture that assure us that God does answer prayer. ". . . If you, then, though you are evil, know how to give good gifts to your children, how much more will your Father in heaven give good gifts to those who ask him!" (Matt. 7:11).

We learn a number of characteristics of Christian prayer. This may not have been the *primary* purpose of this parable; but, it is certainly taught. Four characteristics of Christian prayer are: (1) Prayer is an *obligation*. The word is δειν (*dein*, meaning "it is necessary"). Prayer is an *ought* — we ought to pray. Isn't it interesting to note that Jesus — God's Son, one who participated in the creation of all things — prayed in all of his major crises? We certainly believe that major crises were not the only times that Jesus prayed. We also ought to pray always — never cease being a praying person (cf.

1 Thess. 5:17, "pray continually"). (2) Our prayers must be sincere. This certainly describes the petitions of the woman in this parable. She wanted her appeals granted; she was sincere in her request to the judge. Insincerity in prayer is a major characteristic of hypocrisy. (3) Our prayers must be persistent. "Pray continually," or as other translations say, "pray without ceasing." The Lord is not interested in seeing us crawl to Him, but God does want us to be fervent enough in our prayer life that we will not give up on Him. Even as earthly parents, don't we appreciate the persistence of our children when they ask us to bless them? (4) Our prayers will be answered if we ask in faith. Many of us may be guilty of having a lack of faith, and then when our prayer is not answered, we say or think, "well, I didn't think I would get it anyhow!" Have you ever asked for a sick person to be healed and then responded with astonishment when the prayer was answered?

We reach our ultimate potential through our prayers to God. Someone once said that "Man's extremity is God's opportunity." We must reach the place of dependency upon God. Prayers should be asked with a sincere belief that God alone can fulfill our request, and then follow those prayers with diligent obedience or effort as though we had to do it ourselves. This kind of cooperation with God will provide powerful results.

The woman in the parable continued her request because she had faith that it would be answered. When you pray, do you truly believe that it will be answered? I can look to many instances in my own life where I know that God has answered my prayer — there is no other way that some things I have experienced could have happened, except through God's intervention. If we truly believe, God will answer our prayers.

"Learning to Live" from this Parable

There are a number of ways that this parable has helped me to become a better servant of God. Only two of these will be given here, for some of the others will be included in my discussion of other parables.

First, *we should remember that God does not get in a hurry.* We are time-bound creatures. All of our lives are controlled and limited by time. We set goals; we establish limits which involve time. But God is beyond time. He can look at all of time and see it all as though it were the present. He does not get in a hurry. Remember when He promised to destroy the Amalekites in the Old Testament? He chose to take hundreds of years to accomplish that promise. He promised Adam and Eve that one would come "to bruise the head of the serpent" for deceiving them; yet He waited several millennia to accomplish that promise through the coming of Jesus. Be patient with God's responses. Often, the delays may be to help us to develop patience.

Second, *I am reminded of Jesus' penetrating question, Will the Son of Man find faith when He returns?* (Luke 18:9). Isn't this an interesting ending to the parable? At first glance, one asks, "what does this have to do with the persistent woman's plea to the judge?" But when you see the parable in its totality, it makes great sense. The parable teaches us that we must trust God even though we do not readily understand what He is doing. Do I have faith? Do you have faith? We sometimes fret about whether or not God will do what He says He will do. But Jesus reorients our thinking: the question is *not* "Is God faithful?" (He is infinitely faithful.) The question is, "Are *we* faithful?" Will the Lord find faith in you and me? This is one of the pivotal issues taught by this parable.

CHAPTER NINE

Endnotes for Chapter 9

[1] Simon J. Kistemaker, *The Parables of Jesus*, p. 251, footnote.

[2] Arndt & Gingrich, *A Greek-English Lexicon*, p. 848.

[3] Wenham, *The Parables of Jesus*, p. 190.

PRAY TO BE SEEN, OR HEARD?
10

The Parable of the Pharisee and Publican: Luke 18:9–14

To some who were confident of their own righteousness and looked down on everybody else, Jesus told this parable: "Two men went up to the temple to pray, one a Pharisee and the other a tax collector. The Pharisee stood up and prayed about himself: 'God, I thank you that I am not like all other men — robbers, evildoers, adulterers — or even like this tax collector. I fast twice a week and give a tenth of all I get.'

"But the tax collector stood at a distance. He would not even look up to heaven, but beat his breast and said, 'God, have mercy on me, a sinner.'"

"I tell you that this man, rather than the other, went home justified before God. For everyone who exalts himself will be humbled, and he who humbles himself shall be exalted" (Luke 18:9–14).

This parable was spoken after Jesus had given the Parable of the Persistent Widow. The circumstances and purposes of this parable are, therefore, somewhat similar to that already discussed in the previous chapter. You may want to turn back to the previous chapter and read the first few pages.

The parable involving the persistent widow showed, among other things, the need to persist in our prayer life to God. He always listens. He answers our prayers, but not always for exactly what we ask nor in the time frame in which we expect them to be answered. In fact, we might consider this question: Are we always ready to receive God's answer to our prayers? Or would we sometimes find God's answer very inconvenient to our life plan?

In our current parable, Jesus is more interested in teaching us the attitude we should have toward God as we pray. We shall notice two individuals and their radically different attitudes, as clearly illustrated by Jesus.

Background Information

There are two main characters in the story: the Pharisee and the tax collector or Publican. Each represents two well-known groups of people of Jesus' day. In order to understand the force of Jesus' message, we need to note some of the religious, social, and political conditions of that day.

The first character is the Pharisee. Recall that the Jewish people had developed a number of "sects" or groups, depending on their theological, and perhaps socio-political positions on a number of issues. There were at least five major sects: Pharisees, Sadducees, Essenes, Herodians, and Zealots. Each of these groups had a definite influence on the thinking of the people of that time, and each must have come into contact with Jesus on many occasions. Although it would be interesting for us to look at each of these groups, only the Pharisees will be discussed here. For information about the different groups, you may want to read articles from Bible dictionaries or encyclopedias on these five "parties." A casual reading of the New Testament will show that these different groups played a major role in the life and teachings of Jesus.

The Pharisees arose sometime after the Babylonian Captivity. They believed in the law of Moses, but prior to Jesus' birth, they had developed a significant amount of traditional beliefs, or interpretations, of the law. These are generally referred to as the "traditions" of the Jews. When Jesus lived, these traditions were orally passed down from generation to generation. In the early second century A.D., the traditions were gathered together into a collection, now known by the name "Talmud." They have been very influential in Jewish studies through the centuries. The Pharisees believed in many things that Christians believe in, such as angels, spirits, and a resurrection from the dead. However, Jesus regarded the Pharisees as strongly tradition-bound, and He confronted and debated them on many occasions.

The Pharisee of this parable could probably have written a rather impressive resumé. He was obviously a devoutly religious man. Jesus Himself told his followers that the Pharisees taught the right things (see Matt. 23:2–3), but teaching the right things is not enough. As he was describing his life before he accepted Christ, Paul identified himself as a Pharisee to show his religious fervor and dedication (see Acts 23:5–8; Phil. 3:4–6). The Pharisees were one of the strictest, most legalistic sects of the Jewish religion. This particular Pharisee appears to be a decent and upright man, and it appears that he was financially secure. But his personal flaws included his lack of self-abasement. He also had the wrong attitude toward his fellows.

The second character of our parable was the tax collector or publican, the τελώνης (*telones,* a tax collector or revenue officer).[1] Publicans were among the most despised Jewish citizens. For obvious reasons, tax collectors are rarely among the most respected people. But in the political situation of Jesus' day, there was even greater reason for them to be despised. They weren't really the tax assessors as the IRS and others are in the United States. They were strictly tax collectors. The Romans had developed an unusual way of selecting tax collectors. The following is a fair representation of the office.

> In Judea, under the [Roman] system, all circumstances combined to make the publican the object of bitter hatred. He represented

and exercised in immediate contact, at a sore spot with individuals, the hated power of Rome. The tax itself was looked upon as an inherent religious wrong, as well as civil imposition, and by many the payment of it was considered a sinful act of disloyalty to God. The tax-gatherer, if a Jew, was a renegade in the eyes of his patriotic fellows. He paid a fixed sum for the taxes, and received for himself what he could over and above that amount.[2]

Although we do not know very much about this particular publican, we do know that he was a despised person, simply because of his profession. Jesus often identified the publicans with unsavory or undesirable persons: ". . . treat him as you would a pagan or a tax collector" (Matt. 18:17); ". . . I tell you the truth, the tax collectors and the prostitutes . . ." (Matt. 21:17). The Pharisees identified the tax collectors with sinners: "'Why do you eat and drink with tax collectors and sinners?'" (Luke 5:30). These references are sufficient for us to see the general feeling of people toward the publicans.

Because this man was a publican, it is possible that he was an extortioner. This was the practice of many publicans. However, his prayer and his attitude are represented by Jesus as much more benevolent toward his fellow human beings than were the prayer and attitude of the Pharisee. Jesus used this parable to teach us that we should be humble when we pray to the God of the Universe.

Explaining the Text

This parable is a commentary on real life. The Pharisee was proud of his many accomplishments. In fact, some have suggested that this "prayer-time" provided an opportunity for the Pharisee to tell God how great he, the Pharisee, was and that it was not a prayer at all. Jesus says that he "prayed about himself" (Luke 18:10, NIV); another translation is "The Pharisee stood and prayed thus with himself. . ." (RSV). Prayer is never a time to exalt oneself; it is the deeply personal communion of a frail, finite human being with the eternal, infinite God of all creation. The publican, on the other hand, showed deep humility in his prayer.

Jesus addressed this parable to "some who were confident of their own righteousness and looked down on everybody else." Two thoughts from this are: first, "confident of their own righteousness" (from πεποιθότας ἐφ'ἑαυτοῖς, *pepoithotas eph'heautois*, literally meaning to "put one's confidence in himself"); the second thought is "looked down on everybody else (from ἐξουθενοῦντας, *exouthenountas*, "to consider or treat as nothing").

The Pharisee told God that he fasted twice a week. The law stipulated that the Jewish people fast once a year, on the Day of Atonement (Lev. 16:29ff.). But the Talmud gave directions to fast two days a week. Perhaps this is why the Pharisee practiced his regular fasting. He also praised himself for giving a tenth of all he "gets." However, you may recall that God called for a tenth of what a person possessed.

Purpose and Application

The purpose of this parable is evident: Since Jesus addressed this to "Some who were *confident of their own righteousness,*" He wanted to show those who were self-righteous and those who looked down on others what the real meaning of humility is. Prayer simply seems to be the medium through which the Pharisee complimented himself. In teaching the people about humility, Jesus also taught them a powerful lesson on how to pray. In fact, it would be helpful if all of us who follow Christ could take some lessons from Christ on how to pray. How does this parable apply to our learning how to pray?

First, *we learn that humility is a key ingredient for prayer as it is for all of life.* Unless we realize our total dependence

115

upon God, we cannot recognize the *need* to pray. I remember trying to explain to a young man in Michigan many years ago who God is and why he needed God. I told him that God is our Father. He replied that if God was like his father, he wanted no part of him. "Besides," he said, "what can God give me that my wealthy dad cannot give me?" This young man had not come to realize his need for God. Is it possible that, in our day of prosperity, many of us have lost the sense of our need for God? After all, we can purchase nearly everything that we want; so what need have we of a heavenly Father? Someone said, as we indicated earlier, that "Man's extremity is God's opportunity." The reason the tax collector "went home justified before God" (Luke 18:14) was that he recognized the "bankruptcy" of his life — he humbled himself and confessed his weakness and need to God.

Second, *through the use of contrast, this parable teaches us the difference between the Pharisee's prayer and the Publican's prayer.* We actually see two contrasts in Jesus' story: the prayers of the two men and the rewards of the two men. The prayers of the two men are easily contrasted. First, the Pharisee's prayer has four characteristics: (1) It indicated no real reverence or humble respect for God. In fact, it almost sounds like he is trying to "sell" himself to God. (2) As the Pharisee prayed, He appears to be trying to forget his humanity and his mistakes. How can sinful human beings pray to an all-powerful, all-knowing God without realizing their terrible humanity? (3) He does not really ask for anything nor does he praise or thank God; he only parades his own "great qualities." He thinks only of self. Notice the number of times in this brief prayer that he mentions himself — at least four times! (4) He actually confessed others' sins — those of the publican — rather than his own. Second, notice that the publican's prayer has at least three characteristics: (1) It demonstrates true reverence for God. Even though he was a sinner and perhaps even an extortioner, he recognized his terrible need for God. He was so distraught that he would not even look heavenward. (2) He openly confesses his own sinfulness. Most of us don't have to be reminded that we are sinners — we know that already. Our problem so often is that we don't want to *admit* our weakness. (3) He begged for mercy. God is the God of mercy. Our faithful obedience will cause God to shower His mercy on us through the cross.

What were the rewards for these two men? The Pharisee did not really ask God for anything. We can't expect our earthly parents to answer our requests if they do not know what we want or need. The same is certainly true with God. God wants us to make our prayers and supplications known to Him. The Pharisee, according to Jesus, was humbled: "Everyone who exalts himself will be humbled" (Luke 18:14). The publican "rather than the other, went home justified before God. . . . and he who humbles himself will be exalted" (Luke 18:14). Jesus warned against our praying "to be seen by men" (Matt. 6:5–8).

"Learning to Live" from this Parable

Do you ever wonder if God is listening to you? Have you prayed only to finish your prayer with an empty feeling? If so, you are not alone; many others feel the same. It is humbling for us to contemplate the enormous world in which we live and try to compare ourselves to people who appear to be far more brilliant or capable than we are. How much more are we brought low when we realize the greatness of God? When I read Psalm 8, I recognize my abject nothingness; but it also gives me hope that God *does* care for me. In these concluding paragraphs, we will note two great ways that studying this parable can help us in our daily lives.

First, *we learn that a sincere prayer requires humility.* Jesus' washing of the disciples' feet was to teach them the importance of serving others and forgetting themselves. If we will but "consider others better than self" (Phil. 2:3), we can put our own lives into better perspective. I can't remember a time when I have forgotten myself to help someone else that I haven't been blessed more than the one I helped.

Second, *we must remember that a person's prayer is answered on the basis of the state of his/her heart rather than on the number of legal codes obeyed.* Don't misunderstand! This statement does not give license to anyone to avoid obeying God's will. Jesus clearly declared that "If you love me, you will obey what I command" (John 14:15). But let us *never* become so bound to legalism that our hearts and lives cannot reach out to others in their needs. The Pharisee undoubtedly obeyed the oral traditions of his father; but he forgot the need to put his own life in submission to God. It ought to go without saying, but we will say it again: *pray to be heard by God, not to be seen by men!*

Endnotes for Chapter 10

[1] See Arndt & Gingrich's lexicon.

[2] Louis Mattthews Sweet, "Tax," *International Standard Bible Encyclopedia,* ed. James Orr (Grand Rapids: Eerdmans, 1955), Vol. V, p. 2920.

KEEP ON WATCHING
11

The Parable of the Keeper of the Door: Mark 13:32–37;
Luke 12:35–40

"No one knows about that day or hour, not even the angels in heaven, nor the Son, but only the Father. Be on guard! Be alert! You do not know when that time will come. It's like a man going away: He leaves his house in charge of his servants, each with his assigned task, and tells the one at the door to keep watch.

"Therefore keep watch because you do not know when the owner of this house will come back — whether in the evening, or at midnight, or when the rooster crows, or at dawn. If he comes suddenly, do not let him find you sleeping. What I say to you, I say to everyone: 'Watch!'" (Mark 13:32–37).

"Be dressed ready for service and keep your lamps burning, like men waiting for their master to return from a wedding banquet, so that when he comes and knocks they can immediately open the door for him. It will be good for those servants whose master finds them watching when he comes. I tell you the truth, he will dress himself to serve, will have them recline at the table and will come and wait on them. It will be good for those servants whose master finds them ready, even if he comes in the second or third watch of the night. But understand this: if the owner of the house had known at what hour the thief was coming, he would not have let his home be broken into. You also must be ready, because the Son of Man will come at an hour when you do not expect him" (Luke 12:35–40).

The first funeral service that I recall attending was nearly fifty years ago. I do not remember much of what was said, but I vividly recall the central idea of that funeral sermon.

The preacher declared, in essence, "Watch for you do not know the day nor the hour of the Lord's return." Jesus did not expect us to stand gazing into the heavens watching, for His coming. Rather, He means for us to be ready when He comes."

Although some scholars of the parables do not believe that these two passages are a parable, they do not and cannot deny the tremendous force of Jesus' teaching here. Also, the similarity of the messages of the two scriptures is evident. It is true that they are not parables in the strictest sense of the term;[1] however, Luke makes this statement, "Peter asked, 'Lord, are you telling this parable to us, or to everyone'" (Luke 12:41). More about these two texts in the third section below. We will treat these two passages as a parable even though they differ in form from other parables.

Background Information

Luke is not as specific in establishing the background as Mark. Mark places this incident immediately after Jesus' prediction of the destruction of the temple, of the fall of Jerusalem, and of the end of the age. Undoubtedly, the major purpose of Jesus giving this parable, after warning them of the impending destruction of the city of Jerusalem and of the end of the world, was to encourage His disciples to always be prepared for His return.

The timing of this teaching is quite significant. It takes place during the very last days of Jesus' life on earth. Such a pointed warning as this might not have occurred in the earlier days of His personal ministry. However, at this time, He is much more intensive in His teaching, since he has so little time to prepare them for His departure and the coming of the Holy Spirit as their Comforter.

Wenham is careful to emphasize that "the main point of

the parable is unmistakable: it is about the importance of 'keeping awake' . . . and being ready to welcome the master when he comes and knocks."[2] The next several days of Jesus' life will be very trying for His disciples. They will see their Master arrested, treated shamefully, mocked, and finally condemned to die. They will be totally confounded at His departure and utterly astonished at His resurrection. Jesus is preparing them for the time to come; but He also wants them to be prepared to *wait and watch* for His second return at the end of the world — a time that neither He nor the angels of heaven know, only the Father.

Explaining the Text

This "parable" is a difficult one in many ways. It has been included in this volume because it imparts an extremely important discipleship concept: constant preparation for the coming of Christ. Although Mark is frequently the basic text, I have chosen to include a text from Luke, which is pertinent to the study. Both of these references — from Mark and Luke — are included together here because of the similarity of language and the message that they give us. Both texts tell of the return of the Master to a wedding feast, but the one from Luke identifies the Master as *serving* at the feast, not merely being the host with servants to do all the serving.

Both texts indicate servants (from δοῦλος, *doulos*, literally "a slave") were assigned the task of watching for the Master's return. Luke refers to "men waiting for their master to return" (vs. 36), and then identifies them as "those servants whose master finds them watching when he comes" (vs. 37).

These four watches of the night are mentioned in Mark 13:35: ὀψέ, *opse*, evening; μεσονύκτιον, *mesonuktion*, midnight; ἀλεκτοροφωνίας, *alektorophonias*, "the crowning of the cock, or at cock crow," or dawn; and πρωί, *proi*, "morning, or early in the morning." H. Porter defined "Watch" as

> A division of the night. The night was originally divided into three watches Jgs. 7:19), but later into four, as we find in the NT (Mt. 14:25; Mk. 6:48). We do not know the limits of the watches in the first division, but the middle watch probably began two hours before midnight and ended two hours after. The fourfold division was according to the Roman system, each of which was a fourth of the night.[3]

Luke mentions only two of these watches: the second and third. But the meaning of the Mark and Luke references is the same — the servants are to be ready in whatever "watch" that the Master may come.

The slaves, or watchmen, were told to "watch" (from γρηγορεῖτε, *gregoreite*, "stay awake"). This was not, as we noted in the first paragraph, an admonition to stand watching; but rather to be prepared; be doing what you are expected to be doing when He comes.

Purpose and Application

There is a need for constant preparedness. Jesus emphasized in both of the references that we must be prepared, for even He does not know when He is returning. We are reminded so often in our turbulent society of the cheap price many place on life. Murders are committed daily throughout our nation for trivial reasons. Life is cheap to so many. At the very moment I write these words, the nation's attention is focused on a very high-profile person who is being investigated for two senseless murders. Jesus regarded life as extremely precious — so precious that we should live in a state of constant preparedness for His return in order to not lose our life. Joachim Jeremias describes the importance of "suddenness" in our present parable:

... The sudden coming of the bridegroom (v. 6) has its parallels in the sudden downpour of the flood, in the unexpected entry of the thief, or in the unlooked-for return of the master of the house from the feast or the journey. The common element of suddenness is a figure of the unexpected incidence of catastrophe. The crisis is at the door. It will come as unexpectedly as the midnight cry in the parable, "Behold the bridegroom cometh."[4]

All too often in our relatively ordered world, we forget that everything we see will someday be totally destroyed, and we will be called to meet the Judge and answer for our deeds. The reality that Jesus will return should stress the urgency of this parable.

The time of the return of Jesus is not known — except by the Father. From the time of Jesus' ascension into heaven, would-be prophets have been trying to predict the day of His final return. At the turn of the first millennium, just prior to 1000 A.D., some soothsayers were warning that Jesus was about to return. In almost every generation, there are similar predictions. As we move closer to and then beyond 2000 A.D., many will be predicting that *this* is the time. But Jesus declared, "No one knows about the day or hour, not even the angels in heaven, nor the Son, but only the Father" (Mark 13:32; see also Luke 12:40). If we accept these statements as true, then how can any person in any age declare that they know? This lesson also correlates with the previous one, that we must be on constant alert!

Jesus has assigned us to keep watch over His house until He returns. Surely the church is the house over which Jesus wants us to keep watch. Each Christian — with his/her own individual abilities — must keep watch over that house. None of us has the same abilities; but each has the same responsibility to protect and promote the Lord's house until He returns. Whoever is a reliable person will be amply blessed by the Master. Luke explicitly states that we will "recline at the table and [Jesus] will come and wait on them" (Luke 12:37).

"Learning to Live" from this Parable

Does this parable have any relevance for us today? Our society seems to believe that everything will continue on as it is today. But, as surely as Jesus came to earth two millennia ago, died, was raised from the dead and ascended to heaven, just that surely will He come again! This parable is as relevant to us today as it was for those who lived when Jesus first declared these truths!

As "keepers of the door," we must do what we are capable of doing. Jesus does not expect any of us to be a superman or a superwoman who can do everything. But He does expect us to do what we are capable of doing. In a parable that we will study later (the Parable of the Talents), Jesus expected all servants to be productive — *even* the one-talent man! The Creator has made each of us as *unique creatures.* There are really no two people in the world who are exactly alike — even down to our fingerprints! Each of us has been given the talents or abilities to do certain things. We can't all be preachers, or teachers, or many other things. But we all have our own abilities. If we put those abilities to work, we will be rewarded!

We must be careful that we are not caught napping when the Lord returns. "If He [the Master] comes suddenly, do not let him find you sleeping" (Mark 13:36). When Jesus found His apostles sleeping when He returned from praying in the Garden of Gethsemane (cf. Matt. 26:36–45), He was greatly disappointed. If He finds us sleeping when He returns to claim His bride, the church, He will be much more than disappointed. He has promised that we will not be admitted to His marriage feast. In the words of Simon Kistemaker,

Once more the servants who have waited for their master to return are commended. The servants have fulfilled what was expected of them: to wait for their master's return. Likewise, all believers, not just the disciples of Jesus, are told to be ready, to watch for and await their Lord's return. If they are dressed and ready for service with their lamps burning brightly in the dark night, the Lord will not withhold his reward when he comes.[5]

May God help all of us to recognize the gravity of the situation. May He help each of us to learn to live the great lessons of this parable and be on watch to protect and promote His great church. In a real sense, we — Christians — are the only "hands" through which the Lord does His work today, and we are the only "feet" that will carry His message to a lost and spiritually starving world.

Endnotes for Chapter 11

[1] See earlier on pages 8–9 for our definition of a parable.

[2] Wenham, *The Parables of Jesus*, p. 72.

[3] H. Porter, "Watch," *International Standard Bible Encyclopaedia*, ed. James Orr (Grand Rapids: Eerdmans, 1955), Vol. V, p. 3074.

[4] Joachim Jeremias, *The Parables of Jesus*, 2nd ed. (New York: Charles Scribner's Sons, 1972), p. 53.

[5] Simon Kistemaker, *The Parables of Jesus*, p. 118.

LOST AND FOUND
12

The Parables of the Lost Coin and the Lost Sheep: Luke 15:1–10

Now the tax collectors and "sinners" were all gathering around to hear him. But the Pharisees and the teachers of the law muttered, "This man welcomes sinners and eats with them."

Then Jesus told them this parable: "Suppose one of you has a hundred sheep and loses one of them. Does he not leave the ninety-nine in the open country and go after the lost sheep until he finds it? And when he finds it, he joyfully puts it on his shoulders and goes home. Then he calls his friends and neighbors together and says, 'Rejoice with me; I have found my lost sheep.' I tell you that in the same way there is more rejoicing in heaven over one sinner who repents than over ninety-nine righteous persons who do not need to repent.

"Or suppose a woman has ten silver coins and loses one. Does she not light a lamp, sweep the house and search carefully until she finds it? And when she finds it, she calls her friends and neighbors together and says, 'Rejoice with me; I have found my lost coin.' In the same way, I tell you, there is rejoicing in the presence of the angels of God over one sinner who repents" (Luke 15:1–10).

Do you remember losing something and then trying to find it? Perhaps you just mislaid it, or you put it where you thought you could find it; then, later you tried to locate your "lost" object but couldn't find it? Do you remember the frustration with yourself as you diligently searched for your lost article? Surely all of us have experienced this many times.

The fifteenth chapter of Luke is concerned with the lost. Sometimes three parables are seen in this chapter; others see four parables — the lost sheep, the lost coin, the "prodigal" son, and the elder brother. In this study, we will divide the four parables into two chapters: In this chapter, we will look at the Parables of the Lost Sheep and the Lost Coin; in the next chapter, we will study the Prodigal Son and the Elder Brother. These four illustrations are similar in that each describes someone or something that is lost to some extent; each tells us some specific things about the nature of "lostness" and how we can become found. We also see the mercy of God depicted as He receives those who sin against Him. We might add here that Matthew speaks of a man owning a hundred sheep and losing one. Matthew does not treat the statement of Jesus as a parable, but rather as a germ of truth (cf. Matt. 18:12–14). Perhaps Matthew simply gave us the gist of the parable; or it is possible that this was spoken on another occasion. Many speakers and teachers often use the same illustrations on different occasions.

Background Information

These two parables, like most, if not all, of the parables are best understood if we consider the circumstances under which they were delivered. As Jesus gets nearer to his arrest and crucifixion, the conflicts He faces are greater. He has just faced criticism for having healed a man on the Sabbath day who was suffering from dropsy (cf. Luke 14:1ff.). To those who seemed to be "status-seekers," Jesus told of the importance of showing hospitality to those who would not likely repay you for the kindness (Luke 14:7ff). And just prior to these two parables, the Lord has discussed the cost of discipleship and the importance of counting the cost before attempting to follow Him (Luke 14:25–35).

Jesus was not a "run of the mill" teacher: He was the Master Teacher! His methods were not like those of the people of His day. Because of the authority by which He spoke and the attention-getting methods He used, great crowds followed Him. The same is true on this occasion. Luke wrote, "Now the tax collectors and 'sinners' were all gathering to hear him. But the Pharisees and the teachers of the law muttered, 'This man welcomes sinners and eats with them'" (Luke 15:1–2.).

So, these parables arose out of controversy, as did much of Jesus' teaching, and over the accusation that Jesus welcomed sinners and ate with them (Luke 15:2). All of the parables in the fifteenth chapter of Luke were presented to answer this accusation. Jesus made it clear that His mission on earth was to save sinners, and each of the parables tells a different aspect of His mission.

Explaining the Text

In order to avoid confusion, the text of each of the two parables in this lesson will be explained before going on to the next, for each one has some unique characteristics. First, we will look at the parable of the lost sheep. The owner of this flock of sheep was probably not a rich man. Jeremias gives us this insight:

> Among the Bedouin the size of a flock varies from 20 to 200 head of small cattle; in Jewish law 300 head is reckoned as an unusually large flock. Hence, with 100 sheep the man possesses a medium-sized flock; he looks after it himself (like the man in John 10:12), he cannot afford a watchman.[1]

The shepherd was tending his flocks in the open country (ἐν τῇ ἐρήμῳ, *en te eremo*, literally "in the open country" or not in a place of danger).

Shepherds would count their flocks when they came in at night, and if he found one missing, he would likely ask another shepherd nearby to watch his flock while he searched

129

for the missing one. The text states that he will keep on looking (πορεύεται, *poreuetai*, present tense, middle voice, "keeps on looking") until he finds it. It is possible that this shepherd is caring for the sheep of someone else who owns several herds. In that case, a missing sheep would be a very important consideration. "When a sheep is cut off from the flock, it becomes bewildered. It lies down, unwilling to move, waiting for the shepherd. When he at last finds it, he puts it on his shoulders. . . ."[2] It is not strange, when he came home with his new-found sheep, for his "friends and neighbors" to rejoice with him, for some of them are shepherds themselves and know the joy of finding a lost sheep.

The Parable of the Lost Coin has some other dynamics at work. The woman in this story has lost one of ten silver coins that she has. This probably was not spending money, but was a special possession. Kistemaker states that

> These coins were part of her dowry and were worn as ornamental decorations on her headdress. The modern equivalent may be a woman's engagement ring and wedding band with studded diamonds. The loss of one of these diamonds causes dismay, anxiety, and worry.[3]

These coins were not tremendously expensive. Neil Lightfoot wrote that "the coin specified by Luke was a Greek *drachma*, which was almost equivalent to the Roman *denarius*. It was a silver coin, and although worth by our standards less than twenty cents, it was the common wage for a day's labor."[4] Since she did not work outside the home, as many women do today, the only place she could have lost it was in the house; so she sweeps her house until she finds it. Her neighbors, again, will know the prize she lost and has found, so they rejoice with her.

Purpose and Application

This parable illustrates that Jesus wanted to teach the religious leaders of His day the value of every person. It is not only the religious leader whom God wants to save; these tax collectors and sinners also are loved by God, and Jesus came to make atonement for them as well.

These two parables show the tremendous mercy and patience of a loving God and Father. They teach us the value of being saved from a lost condition, regardless of one's station in life. These parables show the joy that is exhibited in heaven when someone is saved. If there is joy in heaven, should we not rejoice here on earth as we witness sinners turning to God?

The Lost Sheep illustrates that some are lost as a result of their own carelessness or ignorance, while the lost coin teaches us that we can be lost through the actions of other people. The sheep did not decide to become lost; it wasn't angry with anyone. It just became silly and careless. It wandered off — oh, so gently — from the rest of the flock and did not realize its lost condition for some time! The lost coin, on the other hand, was lost because of the carelessness or thoughtlessness of someone else. In fact, the coin really had nothing to do with becoming lost. One other observation is that the lost sheep was not lost because it was dead; it simply had lost its guide. On the other hand, the lost coin was not worthless, but the fact that it was "out of circulation," not available for its purpose, proved its worthlessness at that time. I have known people in both of these predicaments, haven't you?

"Learning to Live" from these Parables

These two parables are intensely practical and down-to-earth. You and I are so much like all of the characters in the fifteenth chapter of Luke. We are all lost! The subject of this entire chapter is "lostness" and the joy that God has for us to be found. Note carefully some of the valuable lessons we can put to work in our lives.

We are responsible for the souls of many people while we live for Christ. Notice the opening words of the first parable: "Suppose one of you has a hundred sheep and loses one of them" *(vs. 3)*. Are you your brother's keeper? Are you a watchman? Ezekiel was told, "Son of man, I have made you a watchman . . ." *(cf.* Ezek. 3:16–22). In the same way, God has appointed each of us as "watchmen" over the souls of others. What are you doing to find the sheep who are lost? These parables are tremendously evangelical!

Many Christians are gently, and often ignorantly, led away from God's fold by the power of Satan. The sheep didn't intend to get lost; it just wandered off. Any one of us can become disinterested and become lost. How many people have you known who have moved away from their home-towns and extended family units, perhaps to a large city, and become inactive — just like the lost sheep? They didn't intend to "drift away." As we see the sins of others, each of us is just as vulnerable as they are. See Galatians 6:1.

The one who is lost is as valuable as those who are "found." It is true that the shepherd still had ninety-nine sheep left; but the one that is lost is important at the moment. The same may be said of the woman who lost the coin: she still has nine coins left. Count your blessings! And yet, she searched until she found the lost one. This is what Jesus was telling the Jewish leaders: these lost people are precious in God's sight. We often ask, why is the church not growing? Is it because we have lost our passion for souls? Are we content with the people around us, and just don't look for others? This parable involves evangelism! Leave the comfort of your surroundings, and look for those who are lost.

As the coin was lost due to someone's carelessness, so also we may often be the cause for others becoming lost. We can often offend others without being aware of it; their broken spirits may be the cause of slipping. Often our unkind words, lovelessness, unfriendliness, or forcing our "opinions" upon others can cause them to lose interest. This, of course, does not mitigate their sin for forsaking the Lord; but you and I may be able to prevent such from happening. Be on the look-out for those who are losing interest. We must never become content with "our own little group," but we must be watchful for others who want Christ. A good friend of mine used to say, "Everyone has the right to hear the gospel once before others have the right to hear it many times." Let's go looking for the lost sheep and coins among us.

Endnotes for Chapter 12

[1] Jeremias, *The Parables of Jesus*, p. 133.

[2] Kistemaker, *The Parables of Jesus*, p. 207.

[3] *Ibid.*, p. 212.

[4] Neil Lightfoot, *Lessons from the Parables*, p. 117.

REDEMPTIVE RELATIONSHIPS
13

The Parable of the Waiting Father: Luke 15:11–32

Jesus continued: "There was a man who had two sons. The younger one said to his father, 'Father, give me my share of the estate.' So he divided his property between them.

"Not long after that, the younger son got together all he had, set off for a distant country and there squandered his wealth in wild living. After he had spent everything, there was a severe famine in that whole country, and he began to be in need. So he went and hired himself out to a citizen of that country, who sent him to the fields to feed pigs. He longed to fill his stomach with the pods that the pigs were eating, but no one gave him anything.

"When he came to his senses, he said, 'How many of my father's hired men have food to spare, and here I am starving to death! I will set out and go back to my father and say to him: Father, I have sinned against heaven and against you. I am no longer worthy to be called your son; make me like one of your hired men.' So he got up and went to his father.

"But while he was still a long way off, his father saw him and was filled with compassion for him; he ran to his son, threw his arms around him and kissed him.

"The son said to him, 'Father, I have sinned against heaven and against you. I am no longer worthy to be called your son. Make me like one of your hired men.'

"But the father said to his servants, 'Quick! Bring the best robe and put it on him. Put a ring on his finger and sandals on his feet. Bring the fattened calf and kill it. Let's have a feast and celebrate. For this son of mine was dead and is alive again; he was lost and is found.'

"Meanwhile, the older son was in the field. When he came near the house, he heard music and dancing. So he called one of the servants and asked him what was going on. 'Your brother has come,' he replied, 'and your father has killed the fattened calf because he has him back safe and sound.'

The older brother became angry and refused to go in. So his father went out and pleaded with him. But he answered his father, 'Look! All these years I've been slaving for you and never disobeyed your orders. Yet you never gave me a young goat so I could celebrate with my friends. But when this son of yours who has squandered your property with prostitutes comes home, you kill the fattened calf for him!'

"'My son,' the father said, 'you are always with me, and everything I have is yours. But we had to celebrate and be glad, because this brother of yours was dead and is alive again; he was lost and is found'" (Luke 15:11–32).

This parable is one of the best known and most appreciated parables of Jesus. Perhaps the reason for this is that most of us can relate more closely to the emotions and actions portrayed in the story. Which of us has not, at some time in our life, been tempted to "go off into the far country?" Or, have we become angry when we have worked faithfully but someone who was less than honest or upright received the reward? Has this never caused you a bit of jealousy or ill feelings?

Background Information

This parable is one of the most complex parables, but it has passionate simplicity woven through it. It is complex because one wonders who the central character is. Our first answer is, "the prodigal son." Of course, nowhere in the parable is the son referred to as "prodigal," but it is perhaps quite appropriate to refer to him in that way, because of the way his life turned. Surely Jesus must have had the tax collectors and "sinners" in mind when he told about this son. But, then, there is the elder brother. Is he Jesus' caricature of the Pharisees and lawyers as they criticize Jesus for eating with sinners? And, then, there is the father — the waiting father. Howard Marshall has this comment on this parable:

> Of all the parables this one is perhaps the easiest to interpret in broad outline and yet the most open to a variety of interpretation, dependent on where the main emphasis is thought to lie. In its present context it is meant to illustrate the pardoning love of God that cares for the outcasts; the sinful son is welcomed home by the father and his former status is restored. The central figure is the father, just as in the previous parables the shepherd and the house-wife stand at the centre, and H. Thielicke's famous description of the parable as being concerned with "the waiting Father" is correct. But at the same time the figure of the son is developed; we see his sin and his need, his repentance and his return, . . . It would not be inapt to regard the story as "the parable of the lost sons . . . ," since it emerges that the elder son's relationship to his father is not what it should be.[1]

Further reading in this citation would be helpful. But it is clear that there is some disagreement over what is the real central idea. It is for this and other reasons that the title chosen for this chapter is *"Redemptive Relationships."* As in the previous two parables, lostness and salvation are both central ideas of the stories of Jesus. They all center around being lost and being redeemed. All of us can empathize with the various relationships that are reflected from this family. Surely, Marshall observed, "the parable is ultimately concerned to justify the attitude of God to sinners."[2]

Explaining the Text

If we understand the context of this parable to be the same as the other two, and I see no reason to question this, then it is still a part of the answer to the charge that Jesus "welcomes sinners and eats with them" (Luke 15:2). These three parables (the lost sheep, the lost coin, the lost sons) are unique to Luke in their present form and purpose. Jesus does include some of the principles of these parables in other contexts of his personal ministry.

It would appear that this was a fairly "well-to-do" family, financially speaking. When the younger son — and we must assume there were only two — asked for his "share of the estate" (Luke 15:12), his father gave to him ungrudgingly. The Old Testament stipulated that the oldest son inherited as his birthright a double portion of the estate and the other sons would receive equal shares. They were evidently a Jewish family, and the younger son's stooping to eat "the pods" (κεράτιον, *keration,* "fruits from the carob tree," a Mediterranean evergreen tree) that the pigs ate would be repulsive, since pigs were regarded as unclean to the Jews.

When the son returned home, he was given his former status. He was given a ring for his finger (which was a symbol of authority) and shoes on his feet (which signified that he was a free man, not a slave). The elder brother is pictured by Jesus as a pouting, jealous brother who feels he has been mistreated. It is easy for all of us to feel sorry for the older brother; after all, hadn't he remained faithful to his father and hadn't he consistently performed with loyalty and love? Yet Jesus appears to place him in a questionable role.

The more I study this parable, the more I come to believe that the chief character of this parable is the "waiting father" or the caring father. If you read the parable carefully, you will note that the father is mentioned, directly or indirectly, no less than fifteen times. Perhaps my conclusions come from my accumulated experiences as a father; but the father seems to represent our heavenly Father, who is the father of mercy and the giver of forgiveness.

Purpose and Application

Although this entire text is one single story, we will treat it here as though it were two stories — of the younger brother and the older brother for they depict two different attitudes toward the father in the story. And, in a real sense, these two sons represent different ways that we sin against our heavenly Father. And the "waiting father" presents us with a different lesson.

First, *the younger brother, often referred to as the "prodigal" son, sinned with a complete knowledge of what he was doing.* Here is a case of willful rebellion against his father's wishes. He knew what he wanted, he asked for his part of the inheritance, and he departed to use it as he wanted. No one could tell him anything he didn't already know. He spent his life in riotous living and in the type of behavior which was totally against his father's will.

Second, *the elder brother, on the other hand, had gone through the motions of obedience and doing right all along, but he evidently has the wrong attitude about it.* The Pharisees and teachers of the law were legalists: they were very careful to obey every jot and tittle of the law. Not only did they obey the Torah, but they were also careful to keep the letter of the law as interpreted by the oral traditions, the Talmud. But they possessed an unforgiving spirit. Their spirit appears to have invalidated their obedience to the law. So, this part of the parable is undoubtedly directed at those who would not forgive. This attitude is all too often present among Christians. Jesus said that if we cannot forgive our brother who sins against us, neither will God forgive us (see Matt. 6:14–15). So, in a real sense, these two sons truly represent different types of conditions of being lost.

In *Power for Today*, Steven and Emily Lemley have some very appropriate paragraphs about the elder brother, which I want to include here:

> *Music. . .Dancing. . .Rejoicing. . .Love. . .Restoration. . .*To the
> older brother, this celebration was just too easy. Feeling left out,
> he closed his heart to the two people he probably loved more than
> anyone else on earth. How did all of his "rights" end up so wrong?
> He was wrong when he did not perceive the deeper meaning of
> what had happened: the issue was not "nice" vs. "not nice" or even
> "right" vs. "wrong." It was "life" vs. "death," and life had just
> won! The elder brother had been alive all along, the younger
> brother dead. He needed to know that living in sin is death; there
> is vast difference only the resurrected know.
> He was wrong again when he couldn't see his father's love for
> him. There is no sign here that the father loves the "good" kid less
> — but it's hard for us "good" kids to take, sometimes to see that
> the father loves us *all*. Period.
> Now, "good" kids, let's look a little deeper into our inner lives.
> Deeper still. A little deeper. There! Do you see it now? Sin. Could
> it be that deep down we are wasteful children too? Wasteful of life
> and love?[3]

Third, *the waiting father illustrates the long-suffering
heart of God as He forgives the rebellious son yet pleads for
understanding from the older brother.* Try to relate, if you
will, to the anxiety of the father as he waits for the return of
the erring son. He never gave up. It almost sounds as if he
might have frequently gazed off into the direction of the
departure hoping, just hoping, that his son might return. And
what joy is expressed as the young man comes home! The
sinning son is not even allowed to give all of his prepared
speech before he is interrupted. Then, the father's role
changes when he learns that the older brother is angry and
will not attend the coming-home party for his younger
brother. The father is not counting offenses to see which one
has done the most right or the least good. Both are sons! Both
have a place in this father's heart.

True **Redemptive Relationships** *are illustrated here, as* *this family tries to bring itself back together.* Redemptive relationships are badly needed today in our homes and in our churches. Rather than the church being a family as it should be (1 Tim. 3:15), in many places it has become some sort of a social club. We demand to be "entertained" at the worship program; we participate in and promote only that which we ourselves may be interested in. We no longer are interested in the blind, lame, and poor as Jesus was. We fail to reach out to the lost with the "lifeline" of Jesus Who can save them. Our heavenly Father is constantly reaching out to us to save us; but we who are His ambassadors are not reaching out. Why is the church not growing today in many places? Because our hearts are not consumed with the gospel. The time has come for us to become "the people of the towel" and learn to serve as Jesus did when He washed the disciples' feet. We must become a people who will reach out and help others. Here, the younger son was in dire need of help. He didn't need to be told how terrible he was — he knew that already.

"Learning to Live" from this Parable

This parable is one of my favorite ones, for in it I can see the *real* me. It is always hard for us to look at ourselves and to honestly admit what we really are. Here, I see myself in the "prodigal" son; for I have been rebellious to God. I can know that there is in me a love for what Satan has to offer. And I can know that the all-forgiving God has received me back many times. But I also can see myself in the elder brother. Often I have worked hard to accomplish a worthy task. Yet, when I see others who have not been so dedicated as I *perceived* myself to be getting more "glory and praise" than I was getting, I become jealous and resentful as the older brother did. Can you see these same traits in your own life? Perhaps they are there, but you have not permitted yourself to admit it. Take another look! And also look now at some other lessons you can learn for your everyday life from this parable.

First, some believe that they must "sow their wild oats" before they can fully dedicate themselves to God. I remember, as a boy, hearing of a young man running away from home. Those who were worrying tried to pass it off by saying, "Oh, he is just sowing his 'wild oats.'" That statement bothered me then and I have thought of it often through my maturing years. Remember this: if you *sow* wild oats, you will *reap* wild oats. This is just a law of nature! All of us know of those who rebel against what God wants them to do. They turn to the "pleasures of the world." It is not necessary to sow wild oats, or to behave in sinful ways in order to learn to do right! Many have sowed wild oats. Thanks be to God if good teaching has been a part of that person's life before going astray. Often that trained conscience will be active in bringing him/her back. This was true of the younger brother: he returned as a penitent sinner to ask his father to receive him back. God will receive us back, just as this caring father did; but do not let this be an excuse to live lawlessly.

Second, many of us are like the unforgiving older brother. His condition is one of the worst situations to be in. "How many times shall I forgive my brother when he sins against me? Up to seven times?" Peter asked Jesus (Matt. 18:21). As we will see later, Jesus gave Peter a greater insight into forgiveness. Remember, God will not forgive us unless we forgive our brother his trespasses. How often we have witnessed a brother or sister confess publicly his/her sins only to hear some "elder brother" comment, "I wonder how long it will last this time?" What if Almighty God responded to our confessions of wrong in the same manner? The elder brother showed signs of being unforgiving, selfish, jealous, pouty, arrogant and skeptical. Are *you* like this elder brother? As mentioned earlier, many of us have a soft spot in our hearts for the elder brother. We can identify with his anger. He certainly possessed many admirable qualities: he was loyal to his father; he was a hard worker; he perhaps had been over-looked in receiving accolades for the fine person that he was. All of this is good. But when it came time for him to receive one back who had been caught up in sin, he became prey of the devil and became an unforgiving brother rather than one who would help others.

This parable is about *redemptive relationships!* The church should be a redemptive fellowship for all of us. In the family of God, the church, we have the blessings of love and support. In some ways, the church can truly be thought of as a spiritual hospital. We can bring our spiritual cares to one another and receive balm for the soul. We are admonished to care for one another, to be our brother's keeper, to lift up the weak. "Brothers, if someone is caught in a sin, you who are spiritual should restore him gently. But watch yourself, or you also may be tempted. Carry each other's burdens, and in this way you will fulfill the law of Christ" (Gal. 6:1–2).

Endnotes for Chapter 13

[1] I. Howard Marshall, *Commentary on Luke: New International Greek Testament* (Grand Rapids: Eerdmans, 1978), p. 604.

[2] *Ibid.*

[3] Steven S. and Emily Y. Lemley, "The Elder Brother Was Right (And You Know It!)," *Power For Today*, XXXIX, 1, 1994), p. 2.

CONCLUSION TO PART II:
LIFE AND DISCIPLESHIP

Discipleship is at the very heart of Christianity. Jesus spent His entire personal ministry on earth training His disciples to follow in His steps. He called them from many different walks of life and personally mentored them so they would be able to perpetuate His kingdom after He returned to the Father.

So important was discipleship that some of the final words of Jesus to His disciples were "All authority in heaven and on earth has been given to me. Therefore, go and make disciples of all nations, baptizing them in the name of the Father and of the Son and of the Holy Spirit, and teaching them to obey everything I have commanded you. And surely I will be with you always, to the very end of the age" (Matt. 28:18–20).

The seven parables we have just studied are all centered on discipleship. From "Who is my neighbor" to the wonderful parables of "lostness" in Luke 15, we see Jesus training His disciples to be able to take that same training to all the world. We have seen the attitude that should be displayed by disciples. The important seats at a feast are reserved for those who will be assigned to them by the host; so, we should exhibit the spirit of humility in all we do. There is no place in the kingdom for disciples who seek to find the chief seat, or who will pray to God as though no needs were perceived by the petitioner. Surely we were impressed in the previous parables with the concept of "a people of the towel." We should, like Jesus, be willing to wash the feet of others.

Jesus expects His disciples to be fervent and persistent. The Persistent Widow illustrates to us how we must not become discouraged in our trek to heaven. But we should rely on a God who hears our prayers just as surely and lovingly as a parent hears the prayers of the child. The woman would not give up. Rather, she continued until the unjust judge was willing to grant her the wishes of her heart. Then, there was the Publican and the Pharisee who prayed to God: one in his tremendous penitence and the other out of his self-righteous self-centeredness. Jesus told His listeners that the publican, the sinner, was the more righteous of the two.

What a climax to discipleship is seen in the parables dealing with "lostness." Heaven is watching breathlessly to witness those who were lost but have been found. The woman who lost the coin but found it; the man whose sheep became displaced but was rejoined to the flock. We were told that there is joy in heaven over our overcoming "lostness." The two sons and the anxious waiting father all show the tenderness of our heavenly Father's anxious waiting for us to come "home" to Him.

Discipleship is truly at the heart of Christianity. Jesus wants all of us or none of us! If we are not willing to forsake all and become a disciple of Jesus, He does not want us (see Matt. 10:42). Jesus wants all of you. And for that, His grace is sufficient to sustain us until we are with Him eternally in the home prepared for us.

PART III: GROWTH PARABLES

Jesus was intensely interested in growth. One of the earliest descriptions of the Lord as He grew up is "And Jesus grew in wisdom and stature, and in favor with God and man" (Luke 2:52). It is certainly a law of nature that a living thing either grows or dies. There is no such type of an existence as "standing still." Often we hear people say of a certain church group, "Oh, we're holding our own." This is not possible in the long run. We either grow or die.

Much of Jesus' teaching involves growth. The Sermon on the Mount, one of the central parts of Jesus' teaching, has an underlying emphasis on growth. In these teachings, Jesus stresses the need for personal improvement, both in attitude and action. The Beatitudes emphasize the need for increasing the growth of the inner person. The emphasis on prayer and fasting is to help the individual to develop spiritually. Jesus spent about three years with His chosen twelve with their growth in view. He knew that when He went back to the Father, they would need to be strong. He put them to the test. The early church emphasized spiritual growth as an essential goal. As one reads the Acts of the Apostles, it is important to notice the number of times growth is stressed. In fact, Acts may be divided into six sections, separated by a colophon, or a descriptive statement, which told of the growth of the church.

The parables we will study now have been referred to as "Growth Parables," because they emphasize improvement and enlargement of character and spirit. It is often difficult to decide which are the "Growth Parables," because in one sense, all of Jesus' parables are "growth" parables. However, the ones selected here appear to be more specifically growth-oriented than most of the other parables. Your indulgence is requested as you study these. You might very well have chosen other parables to be included in this group; or you might have preferred to include some of these elsewhere. Our categories should not be regarded as hard and fast; they are simply used to help us to appreciate Jesus' teaching to the fullest.

FROM INSIDE TO OUT
14

The Parable of the Mustard Seed and the Parable of the Yeast:
Matt. 13:31–33; Mark 4:30–33; Luke 13:18–21

He told them another parable: "The kingdom of heaven is like a mustard seed, which a man took and planted in his field. Though it is the smallest of all your seeds, yet when it grows, it is the largest of garden plants and becomes a tree, so that the birds of the air come and perch in its branches."

He told them still another parable: "The kingdom of heaven is like yeast that a woman took and mixed into a large amount of flour until it worked through the dough" (Matt. 13:31–33; see also Mark 4:30–33; Luke 13:18–21).

There are several of Jesus' parables that could be called "companion parables," for they are similar enough to study them together. Some scholars use these similarities as reasons to declare that we do not have the accurate text of Jesus' teaching. "Why else would there be these differences?" they ask. This is really not a valid argument to prove that Jesus did not actually say these things. All of us who are teachers or speakers often use the same illustrations in different situations. We also vary these stories from time to time to fit the situation. It is highly likely that Jesus did this also. An example of this practice can be seen as we compare the synoptic gospels regarding the two parables we are about to study. Matthew, Mark and Luke have some variation in the words they use to tell the stories. But these different accounts of Jesus' parables are not proof of contradiction. These differences are not contradictory; they are merely different.

Background Information

Our two present parables are very similar. The Parable of the Leaven is found in only two of the synoptic gospels; for some reason unknown to us, Mark does not choose to include it in his list of parables. They are presented in the same context as several other parables given at the Sea of Galilee. Jesus delivered some parables to the large crowd which had assembled itself around Jesus, so large a crowd, in fact, "that he got into a boat and sat in it, while all the people stood on the shore" (Matt. 13:2). However, later that same day, Jesus "left the crowd and went into the house" (Matt. 13:36) and continued to deliver other parables to his closest disciples. Our two present parables appear to be the last in the series that He delivered to the crowd on that occasion.

We could have placed these two parables into the category of "kingdom" parables, since Jesus used them to talk about the nature of the kingdom. However, they are included in this grouping because their major emphasis is upon growth. Both of them demonstrate growth from smallness to greatness. At the Sea of Galilee, Jesus had delivered the parables of the Sower and of the Tares, already discussed. The parables of the Mustard Seed and the Yeast depict a more positive, productive picture of the kingdom — one that is growing and succeeding — while the parables of the Sower and the Tares present a somewhat more mixed picture. The Sower shows that many of the seeds fail to prosper, and the Tares discusses how the Devil sowed wild seed among the good seed. But our present two parables discuss the great growth experienced by the kingdom of heaven. As we shall see, the parable of the Mustard Seed represents extensive growth, that is, growth influenced by outside circumstances such as the soil, the rain and the cultivation; the parable of the Leaven, though, represents intensive growth influenced by the nature of the yeast as it becomes a part of the dough as it does its work.

These two parables definitely belong together. Wenham wrote that "There are a number of 'parable pairs' in the gospels. . . . The mustard seed and the leaven are such a pair, the one parable taken from the sphere of men's working (sowing) and the other from the sphere of women's working (cooking in the home)."[1] Wenham is writing out of his understanding of the gender roles at the time of Jesus; however, I am not sure that Jesus was caught up in a gender role as He spoke this parable. It is fair to state that Wenham shares this same feeling. The fact that these two parables find their context in everyday life situations is really what made it easier for the people to understand what Jesus was saying.

Explaining the Text

In the first parable, a mustard seed is not literally the smallest seed in the world, but it was the smallest known to Jesus' audience. The word here is μικρότερον (mikroteron, "smallest") as compared to the phrase μείζον των λάχανον, (meidzon ton lachanon, "larger than any garden plant"). Since Jesus participated in the Creation, He surely knew that the mustard seed is not actually the smallest seed in existence, and there may have been larger garden plants. It appears, therefore, that Jesus is using a pair of hyperboles here to emphasize His point. However, in Palestine, the mustard plant has been known to grow to eight feet or taller. It "becomes a tree," a metaphor for "like" a tree, for the birds to perch in its branches.

In the second parable, the amount of yeast and meal used is unconsequential. The Greek words used here are σάτα τρία (sata tria), or "three measures" of flour. Perhaps this represented the amount that one would normally make. But, it is translated in the NIV as "a large amount" because Jesus wanted to show the powerful effect of the leaven (ζύμη, *zume*, "yeast or leaven"). "Leaven," in Jewish society, often meant something evil because it was associated with fermentation or rottenness. They thought of leaven in terms of wickedness or evil influence. The New Testament often uses the word "leaven" as a symbol of good. Lightfoot says, "Standing either for good or bad, leaven was a figure for any strong or pervasive influence."[2]

Purpose and Application

These two parables are rich with meaning. They very appropriately illustrate the phenomenon of growth. As we stated earlier, they are "upbeat" in their tone, for they speak of a very positive influence. What were the functions of these parables in Jesus' teaching?

Jesus wanted to impress His disciples that, out of such a small beginning, a great kingdom would come — filling the earth. To illustrate this lesson, Jesus showed that the mustard seed would enlarge itself many, many times to become a "tree" or large plant. And He told of the yeast, which would cause the dough to expand to a much larger size than before. So also the church will become much greater through our evangelization. Jesus once told His disciples "I tell you the truth, anyone who has faith in me will do what I have been doing. He will do even greater things than these, because I am going to the Father" (John 14:12). I ask you, what greater thing can we do than healing the sick or raising the dead? Just this: we are able to give people the gospel, which will heal, not the physical body, but the spiritual body.

These two elements (mustard seed and yeast) *each work differently: one from the inside and the other from the outside*. The yeast works from the inside — quietly, unseen — but it does its work. We can think of this as *intrinsic activity*. The mustard seed, on the other hand, is more of an *extrinsic activity*, doing its work out in the open. This reminds us that there are people in the church who work better behind the scenes, without any fanfare; while others are involved in more open, observable situations. Both are equally important, and one should not feel guilty about not being able to do both.

We are victimized by bigness. If we don't have big churches, we think them unsuccessful; if we do not do some big or great work, we often think that we have failed. But God's ways are different than our ways. His word is all-powerful, and it *will* accomplish what He wants it to accomplish. Remember this: the world will be converted to Christ *one person at a time*. God does not have to have great mass conversions; He wants each of us to individually accept Him. The church, or the kingdom of heaven, will fill the earth just as the mustard seed became the roosting place of the birds and the yeast caused the dough to rise. God's word is all-powerful.

"Learning to Live" from these Parables

Life is a process of continual beginnings. Another way of saying this is that we are always "becoming" but we never "arrive." There is no such thing as separating our lives from the events and people around us. We are constantly changing, growing, shrinking, doing, becoming. It is a constant activity in the present tense. The Greeks had a great concept of the present time: they saw the present tense as something that is always in process. This is the way it is with Christians. As the Mustard Seed and the Yeast are continuing to do their job, so we are continuing to make ourselves into the likeness of God.

Christ will produce great changes in our lives if we allow Him to work within us.

The gospel must be carried to others just as the seed had to be planted and the leaven had to be placed in the flour. If the word of God is in us, each Christian becomes a leavening agent. Jesus urged that our lives be examples for others (Matt. 5:13–16). We are the salt that flavors and preserves the world, and we are the light that shines in people's lives to bring them to Christ. The early Christians were busily engaged in taking the gospel to others. After persecution began in Jerusalem, the Christians were scattered, and Luke states that "Those who had been scattered preached the word wherever they went" (Acts 8:4).

The church provides a refuge for all humanity. In the days of the Old Testament, the Israelites had cities of refuge for protection from harm (see Josh. 20:1–9). We flee to Christ for refuge. But, for Him to be a refuge, we must take advantage of the opportunity. For example, the birds were not forced to use the mustard plant. It was there to provide a refuge for them, but they had to take the initiative. Too many of us think that God will take care of us, and we have to do nothing. It is true that we are saved by God's grace; but we have to take advantage of it — we have to eagerly receive that grace. Obedience to Jesus' commandments and trust in Him as a refuge will bring Him into our lives.

Endnotes for Chapter 14

[1] Wenham, *The Parables of Jesus*, p. 55.

[2] Neil Lightfoot, *Lessons from the Parables*, p. 36.

TAKING ADVANTAGE OF MISFORTUNE
15

The Parable of the Shrewd Manager: Luke 16:1–17

Jesus told his disciples: "There was a rich man whose manager was accused of wasting his possessions. So he called him in and asked him, 'What is this I hear about you? Give an account of your management, because you cannot be manager any longer.'

"The manager said to himself, 'What shall I do now? My master is taking away my job. I'm not strong enough to dig, and I'm ashamed to beg — I know what I'll do so that, when I lose my job here, people will welcome me into their houses.'

"So he called in each one of his master's debtors. He asked the first, 'How much do you owe my master?'

"'Eight hundred gallons of olive oil,' he replied.

"The manager told him, 'Take your bill, sit down quickly, and make it four hundred.'

"Then he asked the second, 'And how much do you owe?'

"'A thousand bushels of wheat,' he replied.

"He told him, 'Take your bill and make it eight hundred.'

"The master commended the dishonest manager because he had acted shrewdly. For the people of this world are more shrewd in dealing with their own kind than are the people of the light. I tell you, use worldly wealth to gain friends for yourselves, so that when it is gone, you will be welcomed into eternal dwellings.

"Whoever can be trusted with very little can also be trusted with much, and whoever is dishonest with very little will also be dishonest with much. So if you have not been trustworthy in handling worldly wealth, who will trust you with true riches? And if you have not been trustworthy with someone else's property, who will give you property of your own?

"No servant can serve two masters. Either he will hate the one and love the other, or he will be devoted to the one and despise the other. You cannot serve God and Money."

The Pharisees, who loved money, heard all this and were sneering at Jesus. He said to them, "You are the ones who justify yourselves in the eyes of men, but God knows your hearts. What is highly valued among men is detestable in God's sight.

"The Law and the Prophets were proclaimed until John. Since that time, the good news of the kingdom of God is being preached, and everyone is forcing his way into it. It is easier for heaven and earth to disappear than for the least stroke of a pen to drop out of the Law" (Luke 16:1–17).

This parable is regarded by many as the most difficult to explain of all of Jesus' parables. There are several aspects to this parable that make it difficult. Is Jesus condoning the apparent chicanery of the shrewd manager? What is Jesus actually trying to teach with this parable? Is He telling them that they need to put their trust in money (literally μαμωνᾷ, *mamona*, "wealth or money"; this word is sometimes personified to mean an object of worship or adoration)? Or was He telling them to use worldly wealth as a means of gaining friends? All of these and other possible negative questions have been raised. Jeremias and others give several possible interpretations of this passage.[1] Wenham presents this explanation of the problems:

> This [that Jesus is found to be praising a rogue] has, of course, been many Christians' major worry about the parable as a whole — namely that it seems to be setting forward sharp practice in business as an example to be followed; it is because of this concern that those views which offer an honest explanation of the manager's conduct have been appealing to many. However, the worry is misplaced. We have seen in other parables how Jesus has been uninhibited in using dubious characters, such as a thief, to illustrate features of the kingdom, not in any way condoning the morality of the people concerned, but using some characteristics of their operations to make a point (e.g., the unexpectedness of the thief).[2]

These questions are not easy to answer, but in this study we will offer some answers that may help you better understand what Jesus was saying.

Background Information

As is true of most, if not all, of Jesus' parables, this story could have been a true one that He and even his listeners knew about. Whatever the setting for this parable may have been, it was addressed to his disciples (vs. 1). Apparently the Pharisees were in such a situation so they could hear what He was saying, for Luke states that "The Pharisees, who loved money, heard all this and were sneering at Jesus" (Luke 16:14).

It is highly likely that no change of scene takes place between this parable and the ones mentioned in the previous chapter of Luke. In fact, some believe that there is a connection between the Parable of the Prodigal Son and this parable, in that both the Prodigal and the Shrewd Manager had wasted money: the Prodigal wasted his own money while the Manager wasted others' substance. Some students of the parables contend that this parable is placed at this point in the narrative by Luke because of the similarity rather than of the time sequence. After all, the next parable in Luke is the Parable of the Rich Man and Lazarus, and it deals with wealth. Of course, this is mostly conjecture and may not have been in the mind of Jesus at all. However, the similarity causes one to think about it.

Explaining the Text

This parable is unique to Luke. However, there are many teachings of Jesus that have to do with the management and use of possessions. Someone has estimated that one out of six verses of Scripture have something to do with our possessions and how we use them. I cannot vouch for the proportion of verses that teach about possessions, but a cursory study of Scripture will convince us that it was strongly emphasized. So often we become entrapped by our possessions, and they lead us to do wrong. Paul asserted that "the love of money is a root of all kinds of evil" (1 Tim. 6:10).

Involved in our parable is "a certain rich man" (ἄνθρωπός τις πλούσιος, *anthropos tis plousios*, signifies a man "abundantly wealthy"), who perhaps lived elsewhere, who hired a steward or manager (οἰκονόμος, *oikonomos*, "ruler of the house," not a slave but an important position of power and trust) to manage his household. This man assigned the duties of others; he was the steward and the paymaster for the rich man.

Eventually the manager "was accused of wasting his possessions" (Luke 16:1). "Was accused" is a translation of διεβλήθη (aorist tense, passive voice), *dieblethe*, literally "was accused with hostile intent." So it doesn't appear that the manager just made an error; he was involved with possible hostile intent. "Wasting" is a form of the verb διασκοπίζω, *diaskopidzo*, literally, "to waste or squander." The fact that this is a present participle may indicate that this was an ongoing thing and not just one act of misusing funds. According to Marshall, it could imply neglect of duty or misappropriation of funds, but since there is no suggestion of having to pay compensation, the former is more likely.[3] So, rather than being dishonest, it appears that he may have simply neglected his duty or not fulfilled his duty properly. At any rate, this caused the rich man to demand that he be relieved of his duties. Interestingly, it seems that the dismissal was not immediate, for the steward or manager had time to negotiate the debts owed to his master. Perhaps the rich man was following a practice we generally adhere to today: giving advance notice of termination.

Purpose and Application

One of the difficulties of this parable lies in the way that the manager called in various debtors and arranged a special way for them to settle their accounts. We do not know how he could do this; but evidently the rich man had given him broad powers in managing his accounts. From our viewpoint, this appears to be an "under the table" or dishonest action, but Jesus is not condoning *what* the man did; He simply praised the man for being able "in this world" to deal shrewdly. From this, Jesus told those listening that "people of the light" need to be able to deal shrewdly with our eternal dwellings. Jesus is certainly not commending the dishonesty, lying, stealing or cheating that was done by the manager. The parable should not be treated as an analogy or allegory in which each thing represents something specific. It is vital for us to understand the total thrust of the parable. We might wonder, as we read the parable, if the manager's problem was that he let the accounts or debts get too high and was unable to make proper collections. He may have wanted to be popular and not to press the debtors. Later, then, he "cut a deal" with them for personal gain.

The story is given to teach that *children of the world are wiser in their dealings than children of God in their dealings.* We must be careful here to make the right comparison. The problem is that we become so caught up with the "dealings" of the world that we do not understand what the "dealings" of the children of God really are. Children of the world and children of God have vastly different goals. "Success" for children of the world is not the same thing as "success" for the children of God. "Getting ahead" in one's career, calling, or position in life is a prime goal for children of the world. Living a life that is consonant with Christ's teaching is the measure of success for the Christian. It is essential for us to learn to use our abilities for God as well as the children of the world use their abilities for their own purposes.

Children of God cannot have divided loyalties: it is either God or Satan. Some of those listening to Jesus on this occasion were trying to "straddle the fence." They were lovers of money, and Jesus condemned them for it. It is essential for us to place Christ first in our lives. In this passage, Jesus teaches that "You cannot serve God and money" (Luke 16:13). Wenham has this to say about the purpose of this parable:

> Jesus' teaching in these parables is then: "Invest in the revolution of God," by which he means literal investment. (Or should we perhaps say disinvestment, since it involves giving money away to others?) Just as the dedicated Marxist revolutionary is expected to commit himself and his finance to the cause, in the same way Jesus expects his followers to be practically and not just theoretically committed to the exciting world-changing mission that he inaugurated.[4]

In this way, we can be sure that we have become as wise as the children of this world as we attend to matters concerning "the light."

"Learning to Live" from this Parable

How does this parable affect you and me in the present century? In what is being referred to as the "Post-Christian world," in which you and I are living, can we *really* act in such a revolutionary way as to be wiser than the children of this world? I believe we can! *We must learn to manage our lives, possessions and talents more to the glory of God.* It is so easy in this fast-moving world of ours to become caught up in the trivial. It becomes so easy for us to rationalize a position that is disconsonate with Christ's statement to "seek first his kingdom and his righteousness, and all these things [physical needs] will be given to you as well" (Matt. 6:33).

Many things are important in this life: our families, our jobs, our friends, and more. But *none of these* compares with the supreme importance of placing God first. Until we do this, we are not as wise as the children of the world — for they do place their secular goals in a prime position then labor diligently to reach the goals.

God demands faithfulness of His stewards (see Luke 16:10). "Whoever can be trusted with very little can also be trusted with much, and whoever is dishonest with very little will also be dishonest with much." You and I may not have the greatest abilities in the world; but we *can* use what we have to glorify God. He is far more interested in our willingness than He is in our talent. As the manager in this parable was intent on providing for his future earthly welfare, so we must be careful to provide for our future eternal welfare. The "mammon of unrighteousness" is temporal; but true riches are eternal.

Endnotes for Chapter 15

[1] Jeremias, *The Parables of Jesus*, pp. 45–46.

[2] Wenham, *The Parables of Jesus*, p. 164.

[3] Marshall, *Commentary on Luke*, p. 617.

[4] Wenham, *The Parables of Jesus*, pp. 169–170.

USE WHAT YOU'VE GOT!
16

The Parable of the Talents and the Parable of the Pounds:[1]
Matt. 25:14–30; Luke 10:11–26

"Again, it will be like a man going on a journey, who called his servants and entrusted his property to them. To one he gave five talents of money, to another two talents, and to another one talent, each according to his ability. Then he went on his journey. The man who had received the five talents went at once and put his money to work and gained five more. So also, the one with two talents gained two more. But the man who had received the one talent went off, dug a hole in the ground and hid his master's money.

"After a long time the master of those servants returned and settled accounts with them. The man who had received the five talents brought the other five. 'Master,' he said, 'you entrusted me with five talents. See, I have gained five more.'

"His master replied, 'Well done, good and faithful servant! You have been faithful with a few things; I will put you in charge of many things. Come and share your master's happiness!'

"The man with the two talents also came. 'Master,' he said, 'you entrusted me with two talents; see, I have gained two more.'

"His master replied, 'Well done, good and faithful servant! You have been faithful with a few things; I will put you in charge of many things. Come and share your master's happiness!'

"Then the man who had received the one talent came. 'Master,' he said, 'I knew that you are a hard man, harvesting where you have not sown and gathering where you have not scattered seed. So I was afraid and went out and hid your talent in the ground. See, here is what belongs to you.'

"His master replied, 'You wicked, lazy servant! So you knew that I harvest where I have not sown and gather where I have not scat-

163

tered seed? Well then, you should have put my money on deposit with the bankers, so that when I returned I would have received it back with interest.

" 'Take the talent from him and give it to the one who has the ten talents. For everyone who has will be given more, and he will have an abundance. Whoever does not have, even what he has will be taken from him. And throw that worthless servant outside, into the darkness, where there will be weeping and gnashing of teeth' " (Matt. 25:14–30).

While they were listening to this, he went on to tell them a parable, because he was near Jerusalem and the people thought that the kingdom of God was going to appear at once. He said: "A man of noble birth went to a distant country to have himself appointed king and then to return. So he called ten of his servants and gave them ten minas. 'Put this money to work,' he said, 'until I come back.'

"But his subjects hated him and sent a delegation after him to say, 'We don't want this man to be our king.'

"He was made king, however, and returned home. Then he sent for the servants to whom he had given the money, in order to find out what they had gained with it.

"The first came and said, 'Sir, your mina has earned ten more.'

" 'Well done, my good servant!' his master replied. 'Because you have been trustworthy in a very small matter, take charge of ten cities.'

"The second came and said, 'Sir, your mina has earned five more.'

"His master answered, 'You take charge of five cities.'

"Then another servant came and said, 'Sir, here is your mina; I have kept it laid away in a piece of cloth. I was afraid of you, because you are a hard man. You take out what you did not put in and reap what you did not sow.'

"His master replied, 'I will judge you by your own words, you wicked servant! You knew, did you, that I am a hard man, taking out what I did not put in, and reaping what I did not sow? Why then didn't you put my money on deposit, so that when I came back I could have collected it with interest?'

"Then he said to those standing by, 'Take his mina away from him and give it to the one who has ten minas.'

" 'Sir,' they said, 'he already has ten!'"

"He replied, 'I tell you that to everyone who has, more will be given, but as for the one who has nothing, even what he has will be taken away. But those enemies of mine who did not want me to be king over them — bring them here and kill them in front of me'" (Luke 19:11–27).

These two parables — that of the Talents and of the Pounds (or Minas) — are being studied together. They really are different parables, but there are many similarities between them, and it is easier to study them together than to study each of them separately. These two parables could be included here, under our category of "Growth Parables," or they could be considered "Warning and Reward Parables." We have chosen to include them under Growth Parables because the emphasis is given to how a person uses his talent, or ability, to the glory of God.

Background Information

There are fewer likenesses between these two stories than there are similarities. Practically the only major likeness between the two parables is their emphasis upon our using what we have to the glory of God, or it will be taken away from us. However, the differences between them make us conclude that they are actually two parables, given to different audiences, on different occasions, and possibly for different reasons. Notice the differences we can see.

The situations surrounding the parables are different. In Luke 19:11–26, Jesus was "near Jerusalem" after having visited Jericho. He had visited with Zacchaeus, the tax collector. As He neared Jerusalem, the people "thought that the kingdom of God was going to appear at once" (vs. 11). The teaching was presented *prior to* His triumphal entry into

Jerusalem. On the other hand, the Parable of the Talents (Matt. 25:14–30), was delivered perhaps three days *after* the triumphal entry into Jerusalem. The Parable of the Pounds is presented to a mixed group of people (see Luke 19:7ff.); however, the Parable of the Talents was delivered to the small group of intimate disciples of Jesus after he had told them about the impending destruction of Jerusalem (see Matt. 24:1ff.). Some critics see the two parables as a contradiction and try to use the differences in them to show the inconsistencies between the two gospel writers. However, there is really no contradiction. It has already been noted that speakers often use similar illustrations with different audiences for various reasons. Jesus simply uses two different, but similar, stories to illustrate lessons to different audiences.

There are differences in the content of the two parables. First, in the Talents, we have a householder leaving home for a time; in the Pounds, a nobleman is going in quest of a crown — obviously two different situations. Second, in the Talents, the talents were unequally distributed: one man received five, another received two and one received one talent; in the Pounds, they were distributed equally. Third, the sums entrusted to the various ones differ enormously in the size or amount distributed to the various servants. Fourth, the rewards that the servants received is not the same in the two parables. Fifth, in the Talents, the "unprofitable servant" was severely punished and cast "into the darkness, where there would be weeping and gnashing of teeth," a much more severe punishment than that given to the useless servant in the Pounds; he was merely deprived of his "pound" or "mina" (NIV).

So, it is true that there are some likenesses when we compare the two parables, but the differences are great enough that they should be viewed as two different parables, delivered on separate and different occasions, to two different audiences. However, it is not an issue over which we should quibble: simply study the parables to learn the message Jesus was giving.

Explaining the Text

There is no reason why one or both of these parables could not have been actual events which Jesus discussed. In keeping with the society of that time, both could have been true. But, we shall leave this to the scholars to discuss.

One of the most important explanations concerning the text involves the two words "talent" and "mina" (or "pound," in some commonly-used English texts). A talent (τάλαντα, *talanta*) is literally "a measure of weight varying in size from about 58 to 80 lb. . . . a unit of coinage."[2] The talent was a sizable amount of money. Lightfoot states that "Originally it was not a coin but a measurement of weight, equal to about seventy-five pounds. In the time of Jesus one talent was worth nearly a thousand dollars."[3] In the case of the Parable of the Pounds, as we have said earlier, the word "mina" (from μνᾶς, *mnas*) was a coin worth about $20.00. So, there was quite a difference in the value of the two coins.

Both of these parables use a form of the Greek word τραπεζίτης, *trapezites* ("a money-changer, banker . . . who accepts no counterfeit money"[4]). However, in Matt. 25:27, the word is translated "banker" and in Luke 19:23, a more free translation occurs with the question, "Why then didn't you put my money on deposit . . . ?" We should keep in mind, however, that banks did not exist in the same way that they exist today. "Money-changer" might be a more accurate accounting of the meaning of the text.

In each of the parables, Jesus used the word δούλους, *doulous*, for the word translated "servants." This word more literally refers to a slave that was owned than to a servant who might have been paid. In each of these cases, the "servants" were *slaves.*

There seems to be a difference in the proportion of the owner's property that was disbursed to the slaves. In Matthew, it seems that the entire property of the owner was divided among the slaves to "take care of" while he was gone. In Luke, there is a definite part of the owner's property that was allocated to be used while he was gone.

Purpose and Application

The two parables are teaching some of the same lessons. It is not the purpose of this study to become highly critical; therefore, we will not take time or use space to try to examine any minor differences in the purpose and application of each of the parables. Instead, we will consider four principles that are suggested as the purpose and application of these parables.

First, *God expects no more of us than we can do.* This is especially illustrated in the parable of the Talents. Jesus said that the master, the man who was traveling and who distributed the talents to the people, "gave five talents of money, to another two talents, and to another one talent, each according to his ability" (Matt. 25:15). Note particularly the last five words: "each according to his ability." God has done the same for all of us. He has given each of us certain opportunities — each according to our own ability. He expects no more of us than we can do. But, He *does* expect us to function to the level of our ability.

Second, *each one of us receives something.* As the old song says, "I may not be able to sing like angels; I may not be able to preach like Paul; but I can tell the love of Jesus. . . ." So often in the church, we tend to become jealous of other peoples' abilities but do not remember that *each of us* has unique abilities that we can use to the glory of God. And, we can be assured that God is not going to hold us accountable for what we cannot do.

Third, *success and failure are judged on the basis of how we use what God gives us.* Thank God, we are not judged in the final accounting by our peers or our fellow-Christians. We would not be nearly as fair in our judgment as God. Notice I said *"how we use"* what God gives us. We can have the greatest of abilities or opportunities but if we do not use them, we will have them taken away and given to another. Each of us will be judged individually.

Fourth, *there will be a final reckoning on the way we have used what God has given us.* There are many statements in God's word assuring us of a final day of reckoning. "Just as man is destined to die once, and after that to face judgment. . . ." (Heb. 9:27; See also Matt. 25:31–46; John 12:47–48; Acts 17:30–31). Christ's first appearance on earth was to bring salvation, but when He returns He will bring judgment to the world. Both of these parables tell us of a day of reckoning on how faithful to God's will we are. It is true that we are saved by grace, but that grace will lead us to obedience of the will of Christ.

"Learning to Live" from this Parable

In addition to the obvious lessons that Jesus intended to be gleaned from these parables (which have been discussed in the last section), there are four ways that we can apply these parables in our everyday lives.

1. *Often, it may be wiser to fail than not to make an effort.* The "one-talent man" and the individual in the Parable of the Pounds who did not try were both rebuked for not having made an effort to invest the money. They were told that they

could at least have given the money to the money-changers, and they could have drawn interest on the money. I believe that the Lord will be more lenient with those who have made an effort to serve Him than those who have not tried at all. Taylor has this to say about the unused talent or pound:

> And this [cast into outer darkness] is to be the end of burying our talent by neglecting our opportunities. Oh, let us be warned in time! for the warning here is given in love, in order that we may be kept from continuing in that course which must have this dreadful result. Never but once, during his abode on the earth, did our Lord blast any created thing; but that was when he came to the fig-tree, looking for fruit, and found thereon "nothing but leaves." He did not blight it into perpetual barrenness because it produced wild fruit, or because it bore poisonous figs, but because he found on it "nothing but leaves;" and so the curse of an eternal withering shall fall at last upon the soul which has done nothing with its opportunities upon the earth.[5]

2. *One must have the courage to "launch out" if he/she expects to succeed.* I remember as a young boy a neighbor whose farm abutted our small acreage. He would come to our house during the winter months and would *plan* the greatest crop for the next year. But I recall that he never was able to bring that crop to fruition. Many of us are like that in the Christian life: we plan to do so much. In our church planning meetings, we have such grandiose plans for how to build the church. But we often lack the faith to launch out with God to bring these plans to fruition. It takes courage to trust that God will help us to succeed. The one-talent man was not willing to "launch out" and take chances with his master's money. It seems to me that God is more pleased when we step out on faith and take some risks than if we live lives of complacency and do nothing.

3. *We often fail because we do not put enough faith in our Lord.* God can do some wonderfully great things through us

IF WE WILL LET HIM. We must trust that He can make us successful. What a statement of faith by Paul as he admonished the seamen on the way to Rome: "Last night an angel of the God whose I am and whom I serve stood beside me and said, 'Do not be afraid, Paul. You must stand trial before Caesar; and God has graciously given you the lives of all who sail with you.' So keep your courage, men, for I have faith in God that it will happen just as he told me" (Acts 27:23–24). Again, ". . . because I know whom I have believed, and am convinced that he is able to guard what I have entrusted him for that day" (2 Tim. 1:12).

4. *We must learn to "use it or lose it."* Anyone who has a skill of any kind knows that if that skill is not practiced, it will be lost. Leave a piece of machinery in the field without using it and it will rust and ruin. A public speaker who does not use that ability will have that ability weakened. An athlete who does not constantly use that ability will "get rusty" and will lose the ability. This is a universal law: we must use our talents or the talents will become useless for us. The Hebrew writer wrote, "Solid food is for the mature, who by constant use have trained themselves to distinguish good from evil" (Heb. 5:14).

Endnotes for Chapter 16

[1] The NIV translates the original work more accurately with the word "mina," but since most of the common translations use the word "Pound," this has been adopted in this text to avoid misunderstanding.

[2] Arndt & Gingrich, *A Greek-English Lexicon*, p. 803.

[3] Lightfoot, *Lessons from the Parables*, p. 172.

[4] Arndt & Gingrich, *A Greek-English Lexicon*, p. 824.

[5] Taylor, *The Parables of Our Savior*, p. 198.

ON SECOND THOUGHT
17

The Parable of the Two Sons: Matt. 21:28-32

"What do you think? There was a man who had two sons. He went to the first and said, 'Son, go and work today in the vineyard.'

" 'I will not,' he answered, but later he changed his mind and went.

"Then the father went to the other son and said the same thing. He answered, 'I will, sir,' but he did not go.

"Which of the two did what the father wanted?"

" 'The first,' they answered.

Jesus said to them, "I tell you the truth, the tax collectors and the prostitutes are entering the kingdom of God ahead of you. For John came to you to show you the way of righteousness, and you did not believe him, but the tax collectors and the prostitutes did. And even after you saw this, you did not repent and believe him" (Matt. 21:28-32).

Have you ever been challenged to do something right, and actually promised or determined to do it, but your good intentions "went out the window"? You probably felt a twinge of guilt, but you were able to rationalize the situation and tell yourself, "Oh, well, someone else will do that." Or, you may have had the opposite reaction. Like the first person mentioned above, you may have had a twinge of rebellion in your heart when you were asked to respond and you told the person that you would not do it. Later on, again, your conscience bothered you and you went out and fulfilled the request. If this has happened to you, then you can relate well to the two brothers mention in the text above. The attitudes of these two sons are very common in our world.

Background Information

The circumstances surrounding this parable occur near the end of the personal ministry of Jesus. The final days of Jesus' earthly life were extremely busy and difficult. The incidents surrounding this parable include four significant events. First, Jesus made His triumphal entry into the city of Jerusalem (Matt. 21:1–11). The crowds witnessing this momentous event were deeply impressed and convinced that Jesus was truly the prophet whom they had looked for (vs. 11). Many asked who He was, and undoubtedly His enemies were inflamed at Jesus' exaltation. Second, Jesus cleansed the temple. This was a bold move on the part of Jesus. However, one should be aware that Jesus did not fight back when He was attacked; but, when His Father God was attacked, Jesus became incensed. There is no doubt that Jesus was angry at the misuse of the temple for money changing and profiteering. Third, Jesus cursed the fig tree because it had not brought forth fruit, and it died. Jesus wanted His followers to realize that each of us has a purpose to fulfill — a fruit to bear. When we are not fruitful, we insult the Master. Fourth, Jesus has His authority questioned. The chief priests and elders demanded that Jesus tell them the source of His authority; He answered with a question that put His questioners in a dilemma. In each of these circumstances, Jesus was faced with conflict. C.H. Dodd makes an interesting observation on the purpose of this parable: "Thus the Matthaean parable of the Two Sons (Mt. 21:28–32) is clearly a comment on the rejection of the word of God by the religious leaders, and its acceptance by the outcasts, as the evangelist represents it."[1] So, Jesus is attacking these leaders for their failure to serve God completely.

Examining the Text

The text in this parable is fairly straightforward. Three

words are used that would be of some interest to the student who wants to analyze the language in more detail. We will look at two of the words together, for they are often treated as synonyms, but with a little different "twist" in their meanings. These two words are μεταμελήθεις (*metameletheis*, to regret or change one's mind) and μετάνοια (*metanoia*, to change one's mind or repent). Only the first of these two words is used in the text. Greek literature suggests that the first of the two words signifies only sorrow for what one has done. But the second word carries with it the concept of repentance. In the instance of the first brother, he appears to be sorry that he told his father he would not go. He was not rebellious; nor was he lying to him; he just changed his mind. Although the word *metanoia* is not used in the second instance, it is certainly implied that the first brother did repent (and the first word above certainly implies "repent") and went. The second brother, on the other hand, said he would go but decided not to go work.

The third word we note is the word προάγουσιν (*proagousin*, literally, "are entering ahead of you"), and it signifies that the tax collectors and prostitutes are going into the kingdom before those to whom Jesus is speaking. This parable is a strong indictment against those chief priests and elders who are challenging Jesus.

Purpose and Application

Strictly speaking, in this parable, Jesus is condemning the formalistic worship of the people of His day because it tended to become void of true obedience. Their attitude toward worship caused them to go "through the form" of worship and feel content that they were serving God. Our own worship often depreciates into that sort of formalistic "rule-keeping" type of obedience.

Jesus is illustrating the real meaning of obedience. It is not sufficient to have good intentions. Someone has aptly said, "The road to Hell is paved with good intentions." Good intentions must be followed with obedience. God did not make us automatons; He created us as thinking, living, decision-making human beings. Jesus appropriately expressed it when He said, "If you love me, you will obey what I command" (John 14:15). Unexpressed love is not really true love. Did the son who promised to work in the vineyard but later refused to do so *really* demonstrate love for his father?

The two sons in Jesus' story represented two different groups of people. The first son who refused his father's request to work but later went represented the "tax collectors and prostitutes" (see vs. 31). The tax collectors and prostitutes were obvious sinners; but when the message of God's love was told, they were willing to change their minds and do right. The second son who graciously consented to go and work but did not go represented the Jewish leaders. They knew God's will, but they allowed their traditions to get in the way of true obedience to God.

"Learning to Live" from this Parable

This is a powerful lesson on discipleship, but it also emphasizes growth, at least in the life of the son who changed his mind and went. Even though we are not worthy, God has called *all of us* to become His disciples. He expects us to work in His vineyard. God knows all of our weaknesses and is able to help us to overcome them.

I called this chapter "On Second Thought." Certainly all of us have developed *second* impressions about many things. Haven't you noticed that many times, our second impressions tend to be better than the first ones? Well, this is probably because we have had a chance to think about the situation and make better conclusions.

We have a God of second chances. How many times has God given people second chances? We can think of Abraham (when he was trying to save Lot's family), Jonah (after he escaped from the fish's belly), and Peter (after his repeated denial of Jesus), and certainly all of humanity who are surrounded by sin. God is truly a God of second chances.

*Jesus illustrates two types of people: the **agreeable** and the **rebel**.* The agreeable people are illustrated by the son who was asked to work in the vineyard and agreed, but later changed his mind and did not go. In the church, there are those who will agree to do almost anything they are asked to do, but then they never fulfill their promises. Perhaps you may be like this at times. Repentance is not just a regret that one has about something he/she has promised to do but did not do; it is a changing of the heart and mind that should result in an actual turning.

The rebel is a person who, for whatever reason, doesn't want to accept responsibility. These people are illustrated by the brother who refused to work in the vineyard, but later repented and went. Maybe we are all like this at times. I know I have seen this kind of person in the church, and I have seen myself in the same light. Why do people respond in this way? Many reasons: we don't like for someone to tell us what to do; we have difficulty following directions; we want to be begged. But, remember: *Jesus wants us all to work in His vineyard.* His death at Calvary was to provide us with that opportunity! Perhaps we could say that there are really two types of people: the "agreeable disobedient" and the "disagreeable obedients." Another way of putting this would be to say there are "saintly" sinners and "sinful" saints. None of us is perfect in our response to God.

Endnotes for Chapter 17

[1] C.H. Dodd, *The Parables of the Kingdom* (New York: Charles Scribner's Sons, 1961), p. 93.

A SOLID FOUNDATION
18

The Parable of the Two Builders: Matt. 7:24–27

"Therefore everyone who hears these words of mine and puts them into practice is like a wise man who built his house on the rock. The rain came down, the streams rose, and the winds blew and beat against that house; yet it did not fall, because it had its foundation on the rock. But everyone who hears these words of mine and does not put them into practice is like a foolish man who built his house on sand. The rain came down, the streams rose, and the winds blew and beat against that house, and it fell with a great crash" (Matt. 7:24–27; see also Luke 6:46–49).

This is not, in the strictest sense of the word, a parable. It is more of a comparison or an analogy. This is actually indicated in the text when Jesus said, "is like. . . ." The Greek text literally says, "I will liken," (from ὁμοιώσω, *homoioso*, "I will liken, or "I will compare"). However, many students of the parables include this in their treatment of the parables. Jesus' teachings are filled with illustrations, stories, parables, comparisons, and other means of making His message more clear. To that extent, this qualifies as one of the "parabolic statements" of Jesus. Luke includes this in His treatment of Jesus, but there are some differences you will note as you compare the two writings.

This is a very well-known passage of Scripture. My good friend, Bill Henegar, shared a statement he made concerning this. He said, "It is unfortunate that a child's song is based upon this text ("The wise man built his house on the rock," etc.), for it may cause us to lose sight of the real importance of the lesson and think of it only as a little 'ditty' that we can sing." It truly is a very significant illustration — one that all of us should consider very seriously as we contemplate the role of Christ in our lives. For, this tells us of the sure foundation that we have by hearing and obeying Christ's words.

Background Information

The setting for this parable is Galilee. It is a part of the Sermon on the Mount, which is generally agreed to have been delivered in view of the Sea of Galilee. In fact, there are two traditional locations where the Sermon may have been delivered: either a mount northwest of Capernaum or else the peak just west of the Sea of Galilee and between Tiberius and Capernaum. When one visits the Holy Land today, the location that is generally pointed out is the latter one. If this was the place, it was an ideal location for the multitudes to sit on the slope down to the Sea of Galilee, and the acoustics are excellent. When one sits a few hundred feet away from the Sea of Galilee, voices can be heard and clearly understood from the edge of the Sea. Regardless of where the mount was, this parabolic statement is a part of that momentous message.

Matthew places this parable as the climax of Jesus' sermon. It is preceded by two very significant and related topics: the narrow and wide gates and the tree and the fruits that it bears. This is one of the most forceful statements that Jesus made enjoining obedience to Him. He clearly states that there are only two ways that people can respond to His teachings and His claims: they either hear and obey, or they hear and do not obey. And each of us has that choice to make. William Barclay wrote that "In this parable Jesus is making a staggering claim. In effect He is saying that obedience to His teaching is the only safe foundation for life."[1] How very appropriate this lesson is to people, like myself, who live in Southern California and witness the hillside slides that demolish houses built on unsure foundations!

Explaining the Text

At first glance, this looks like such a simple, easy-to-understand text. But the lessons it gives us are sublime. Some of the words in the text seem to be selected with great care. For example, there are two actions that are discussed: *hearing* and *doing*. "Therefore everyone who hears" is translated from πᾶς οὖν ὅστις ἀκούει, *pas oun hostis akouei* (literally, "everyone therefore whosoever hears"). The word "to hear" also includes by implication the process of understanding. "And does them" comes from καὶ ποιεῖ αὐτούς, *kai poiei autous*. Richard C. Trench states that this word "brings out more the object and end of an act,"[2] hence showing the importance of the words of Jesus.

One man was like "a wise man" and the other was like "a foolish man." "Wise" is a translation for φρονίμώ, *phronimo*, which means "sensible, thoughtful, prudent, wise."[3] He was not necessarily smarter, just wiser or more "prudent" (according to NIV). The "foolish" man is translated from μωρῷ, *moro*, meaning "foolish, or stupid." This word is the one from which our English word "moron" is derived. This person did not act sensibly, but foolishly or stupidly.

Purpose and Application

As was stated earlier, this is the strongest statement that Jesus made concerning the importance of obeying Him. Earlier in Matt. 7:13–14, Jesus had stated that there are only two gates: the broad and the narrow. Here, Jesus says that those who hear *and* do are wise; those who hear and do *not* are foolish.

These two builders have several points of resemblance. Since this is an analogy, rather than a true parable, note the following five points of resemblance. First, both had heard Christ's teachings. Hence, Jesus is comparing the way that people react who have had equal opportunities. Second, both men saw the necessity of building. Third, both men actually built a house. They did not just plan to build. Fourth, both houses were exposed to storms. All of Jesus' hearers had been and are confronted with fierce storms of life. Fifth, both builders surely felt secure with their structures. Is it plausible to assume that the foolish man actually built a house while knowing that it would not stand the storms it faced? Surely not! It should be pointed out that there is no indication that one house (or life) is better than the other. It was the foundation (or the quality of faith) that really mattered.

Both builders have some points of dissimilarity or difference. First, their personal qualifications differed: as it turned out, one was wise, the other was foolish. Second, their practices differed: one professed to know Christ; the other did what Christ said to do. Third, their foundations differed: one was built upon the sand; the other was built upon a rock. Fourth, their final results differed: one house stood; the other one fell.

There are two major purposes of this illustration from Jesus. First, *Jesus wanted to impress upon His hearers the extreme importance of all He had to say to them.* Jesus was already recognized by the people of His day as a great teacher. In fact, Matthew concludes the Sermon on the Mount with these words, "When Jesus had finished saying these things, the crowds were amazed at his teaching, because he taught as one who had authority, and not as their teachers of the law" (Matt. 7:28–29). Second, *Jesus wanted to impress upon His audience that it is not enough to just hear what He had said. It also must be practiced.* Obedience is vital. Jesus said on a number of occasions that obedience was essential. "If you love me, you will obey what I command" (John 14:15; see also verses 21 and 23). True faith is demonstrated when it is put into practice!

"Learning to Live" from this Parable

Our modern world seems to be turned off by obedience. The existential approach to life seems to be "I'll do it my way; if it feels good, I'll do it." This is *not* the teaching of Jesus. He insists that we must obey His commandments. Four concepts are suggested here if we want to put this parabolic teaching to practice in our own lives.

First, *There is a continual need for self-examination.* We need to ask ourselves, "Why am I doing the things that Jesus commanded? Is it because they seem right to me, or is it because Jesus said for us to do them?" There is a world of difference between these two types of motivation. We are repeatedly admonished in Scripture to examine ourselves. Perhaps the most difficult thing one can do is to look at himself/herself in the proverbial "mirror" to see his/her real person. It is difficult to look at one's own marred self and admit error. But we are taught to examine ourselves.

Second, *it is more important to do all we know than to know more but not do it.* Knowledge is dangerous if it puffs us up so that we do not do anything. Paul lamented the plight of his own people: "Brothers, my heart's desire and prayer to God for the Israelites is that they may be saved. For I can testify about them that they are zealous for God, but their zeal is not based on knowledge" (Rom. 10:1–2). The opening statement of the paragraph is not meant to discourage us from studying. We should all spend daily time meditating on God's message to us. But we must be careful that what we learn from God's word is put into action in our lives. In the verses preceding our text, Jesus said, "Many will say to me on that day, 'Lord, Lord, did we not prophesy in your name and in your name drive out demons and perform many miracles?' Then I will tell them plainly, 'I never knew you. Away from me, you evildoers!'" (Matt. 7:22–23). Obedience is central to the will of God.

Third, *the test of a sermon is found in people's lives, not in what the preacher says*. We can listen to the best sermons ever delivered, but until they are translated into our lives, they are worthless to us. The best translation of the Bible is the translation in our lives. These parabolic sayings of Jesus emphasize the importance of living for Jesus.

Fourth, *the wise man was concerned with inner strength, and so must we be*. We hear much about "church growth" these days. The growth of the church must begin in the heart and life of each individual Christian. Far too many of our trained theologians are able to interpret the minute details of Scripture, but far too many are not emphasizing the role that the Holy Spirit has in the life of Christians. Inner strength is the result of days and years of inner contemplation of the role of God in our lives. Don't let yourself be caught up in hearing *only*; hear and do what Jesus has commanded!

Endnotes for Chapter 18

[1] William Barclay, *And Jesus said: A Handbook on the Parables of Jesus* (Philadelphia: Westminster, 1970), p. 218.

[2] Richard Chenevix Trench, *Synonyms of the New Testament* (Grand Rapids: Eerdmans, 1953), p. 361.

[3] Arndt & Gingrich, *A Greek-English Lexicon*, p. 866.

CONCLUSION TO PART III: LIFE AND GROWTH

When one lives for Jesus, growth will be inevitable because growth is a part of life. In the world of nature, when something ceases to grow, it ceases to live. All of us are comprised of *living* cells. When we read the story of Jesus' life in the Gospel accounts, we learn that He grew. Luke wrote that "Jesus grew in wisdom and stature, and in favor with God and men" (Luke 2:52). The early church "throughout Judea, Galilee and Samaria enjoyed a time of peace. It was strengthened, and encouraged by the Holy Spirit, it grew in numbers, living in the fear of the Lord" (Acts 9:31).

In this group of parables (chapters 13–18) we have been dealing with parables of growth. As we allow Christ to operate in our lives, we will grow. Elsewhere, it has been emphasized that the Christian life is a process of *always becoming* but never arriving at complete maturity; for when we arrive at that complete stage, we will be in the eternal presence of God. This life is a constant process of growing.

There are several aspects of spiritual growth illustrated by this group of parables. Jesus taught that growth is gradual, often unobserved, but in need of external sources acting upon us. This was illustrated in the two parables of the Mustard Seed and the Leaven. Not only was their growth an internal sort of growth, but they represented the phenomenal development that can take place in the life of an individual. Look at Peter! Here is an absolutely astounding illustration of how Jesus' entering into a life can completely revolutionize a life!

Jesus even illustrated growth through the Shrewd Manager who used misfortune to help him in his business development. Although Jesus does not approve of dishonest means of reaching our goals for Him, He told us that we ought to be as wise as the children of the world in our service for God. Each of us can grow into a great person if we will learn to use all of the advantages available to us in our development. Many of us may not have much; we may have limited abilities and limited resources. But the Parables of the Talents and of the Pounds show how we can invest our lives into a growing situation and become very useful for the Lord.

Often, we have to suffer reversals in our lives in order to move forward. This is illustrated in the Parable of the Two Sons. One son was not willing to go work for his father and actually refused to do so. When he further considered, he repented and went. This was a type of growth that many of us are unwilling to accept. Some of the best things that have happened to me have grown out of my rebellion to what I knew was right. Often, we may find ourselves rebelling against God only to repent and actually do what God has commanded.

The final parable of growth centered on the Parable of the Two Builders. How weak our lives often are because we have not built a solid enough foundation of faith. Our whole Christian life is built upon the foundation of faith in God and His Son. When we are willing to take the time to lay the proper foundation in ourselves — and in others whom we are teaching — we will see a long-lasting "building" or Christian life as a result.

Christians must be willing to grow and let Christ grow in their lives. So much is taught in Scripture about growth! Peter expressed it well: "Like newborn babes, crave pure spiritual milk, so that by it you may grow up in your salvation" (1 Pet. 2:2).

PART IV: WARNING AND REWARD PARABLES

Our modern world is reluctant to think of God in terms of warning and punishment. We have grown up in a society that emphasizes the rewards of life and tries to minimize the punishments. It is argued that, if God is "Love," how can He punish us eternally? God is the Creator of all that is. He made us; why would He want to destroy us? it is argued.

Throughout the history of Christianity, and the history of humankind for that matter, some form of "universalism" has been with us. By the third century of the Christian era, there were leading thinkers in the Church who were promoting universalism. Because of the desire of human nature to want the good and avoid the bad, many kinds of universalism or partial universalism have arisen. Some of these theories include such things as purgatory and reincarnation. Even now, in our own time, the New Age movement has arisen promoting the idea that we have come from previous lives and will continue to be reborn into new forms of existence.

In this section, we will be looking at the "Warning and Reward Parables." These parables generally deal with a concept commonly referred to as "Eschatology," from ἔσχατος, eschatos, meaning "last things." Hence, eschatology is the study of end times or last things. The early Christians were greatly interested in last things, especially the second coming of Christ. Paul discussed this in several places. In 2 Thess. 2:1–2, he wrote, "Concerning the coming of our Lord Jesus Christ and our being gathered to him, we ask you, brothers, not to become easily unsettled or alarmed by some prophecy, report or letter supposed to have come from us, saying that the day of the Lord has already come." In his first letter to Thessalonica, Paul also discussed this same idea (1 Thess. 5:1ff.). In verses preceding this, Paul emphasized the second coming of Jesus and encouraged them not to grieve over the loss of loved ones like the ungodly do, for Jesus will come again for both the living who are righteous and those already deceased who have faithfully served the Lord (1 Thess. 4:13–18).

So, it is not surprising that a number of Jesus' parables stress eschatological concepts. In emphasizing warning and reward, the parables in this section stress at least four major topics: 1) Watchfulness, or alertness; (2) Preparedness and stewardship; (3) Fruitfulness; and (4) Persistence. Through some of Christianity's favorite parables, study with us, then, the coming of the end of the world and the need to be prepared for the second coming of Jesus.

THE FINE ART OF FORGIVENESS
19

The Parable of the Unmerciful Servant: Matt. 18:21–35

Then Peter came to Jesus and asked, "Lord, how many times shall I forgive my brother when he sins against me? Up to seven times?"

Jesus answered, "I tell you, not seven times, but seventy-seven times."

"Therefore, the kingdom of heaven is like a king who wanted to settle accounts with his servants. As he began the settlement, a man who owed him ten thousand talents was brought to him. Since he was not able to pay, the master ordered that he and his wife and his children and all that he had be sold to repay the debt.

"The servant fell on his knees before him. 'Be patient with me,' he begged, 'and I will pay back everything.' The servant's master took pity on him, and canceled the debt and let him go.

"But when that servant went out, he found one of his fellow servants who owed him a hundred denarii. He grabbed and began to choke him. 'Pay back what you owe me!' he demanded.

"His fellow servant fell to his knees and begged him, 'Be patient with me, and I will pay you back.'

"But he refused. Instead, he went off and had the man thrown into prison until he could pay the debt. When the other servants saw what had happened, they were greatly distressed and went and told their master everything that had happened.

"Then the master called the servant in. 'You wicked servant,' he said, 'I canceled all the debt of yours because you begged me to. Shouldn't you have had mercy on your fellow servant just as I had on you?' In anger his master turned him over to the jailers until he should pay back all he owed.

"This is how my heavenly Father will treat each of you unless you forgive your brother from your heart" (Matt. 18:21–35).

Forgiveness is an extremely important topic in the teachings of Jesus. This parable could easily be included in one or more of the other categories of parables. However, it is being studied here because of the stringent punishment placed on the unmerciful servant. Eschatology has already been defined as a study of last things; and this parable emphasizes the final disposition that will take place when the unforgiving person appears before God.

Background Information

We know very little about the occasion or location of this parable's presentation. We do know that Jesus had taken Himself away from the crowds. He is evidently speaking only to His disciples (see Matt. 18:1ff.). He is talking to them about various aspects of the kingdom of heaven and certain relationships that they will experience.

Jesus had just taught His disciples how they should respond if a brother sins against one of them (Matt. 18:15–20). This prompted Peter to ask how many times one should forgive a brother when he sins against you. Should it be as many as seven times? Barclay gives us an interesting insight into this question.

> Peter was not without warrant for this suggestion. It was Rabbinic teaching that a man must forgive his brother *three* times. Rabbi Jose ben Hanina said, "He who begs forgiveness from his neighbour must not do so more than three times." Rabbi Jose ben Jehuda said, "If a man commits an offence once, they forgive him; if he commits an offence a second time, they forgive him, if he commits an offence a third time, they forgive him; the fourth time they do not forgive." The Biblical proof that this was correct was taken from *Amos*. In the opening chapters of *Amos* there is a series of condemnations on the various nations *for three transgressions and for four (Amos 1:3, 6, 7, 11, 13; 2:1, 4, 6)*. From this it was deduced that God's forgivenesss extends to three offences and that he visits the sinner with punishment at the fourth. It was not to be

thought that a man could be more gracious than God, so forgiveness was limited to three times.[1]

It is certainly reasonable, therefore, for Peter to ask his question. He knew that his Master was more merciful than the law was; so, he doubled the number of times prescribed by the Talmud and added one. Whether he used the number "seven" because it denoted completeness, we do not know. But imagine his surprise when Jesus responded by saying, "I tell you, not seven times, but seventy-seven times" (Matt. 18:22). The answer provided by the Talmud (three times) was strictly a legalistic interpretation of the law by the rabbis. Jesus' answer to Peter takes this case totally out of the realm of legalism and places it under grace. The grace of God is so broad that it does not count evil deeds. Paul described "love" by saying that "it keeps no record of wrongs" (1 Cor. 13:5).

Explaining the Text

This story involves the depiction of a day of accounting. A king was settling accounts with his servants. Jesus presented a tremendous contrast as He told of one man who owed ten thousand talents and another man who owed only a hundred denarii. These servants are not presented as "hired servants," but as "bondsmen" or slaves (δούλων, *doulon*, plural for "slaves" that were owned rather than hired).

The first slave owed his master ten thousand talents. A talent (τάλαντον, *talanton*) was a large sum of money. Kistemaker says that "the talent in those days was the largest denomination in the monetary system."[2] There is a difference of opinion on the actual value of one talent, but estimates run from $237.00 to $1000.00. Ten thousand talents would have been worth millions of dollars. Kistemaker added that "Herod the Great's annual revenue from his entire kingdom was about nine hundred talents" compared to the ten thousand talents owed by this servant. Clearly, it was a sum far beyond his ability to pay. On the other hand, the second servant owed the first servant a hundred denarii (δηνάρια, *denaria*). The denarius was worth about eighteen cents and represented about one day's wages. So, the contrast between the two debts was huge.

The treatment that each debtor was given is also a great contrast. When the man owing ten thousand talents pled for mercy, the master "took pity" or was "moved by compassion" (from σπλαγχνίζομαι, *splagchnizomai*, to "have pity, feel sympathy"[3]). There is no way that the servant could have been prepared for what followed. The servant merely asked for delay, for the master to wait patiently for him to be able to pay. But the master released him and forgave him the loan. Remember, the amount that the servant owed was far beyond his ability to *ever* pay — it would be equivalent to millions of dollars in our currency, and the servant earned only pennies per day. *But the master forgave the servant!*

One would expect the forgiven person to deal graciously with others. But he "found one of his fellow servants who owed him a hundred denarii" (Matt. 18:28) and he immediately grabbed him (from κρατήσας, *kratesas*, literally meaning he arrested him or forcefully took him into custody) and choked or "throttled" him (ἔπνιγεν, *epnigen*, from πνίγω, *pnigo*, literally meaning "he choked him"), forcing him to fully pay the debt. We are told that, often in Roman courts, creditors were dragged into court by their throats. When the second servant pled for mercy, the first servant put him in prison until all was paid. But when the owner or master heard of this, he called in the unmerciful servant and turned him over to the jailor until *he* paid all of the debt.

Purpose and Application

God expects us to forgive others, if we expect Him to

forgive us. This is so important, for the significant point Jesus made as He concluded the parable was, "This is how my heavenly Father will treat each of you unless you forgive your brother from your heart" (Matt. 18:35). Jesus' purpose for coming into the world was to provide forgiveness for us. The purpose of Jesus giving His life for us was to provide forgiveness for us. Does it not seem logical that He would want us to accept forgiveness as well as to practice it for others? In Jesus' model prayer, He said, "Forgive us our debts as we also have forgiven our debtors" (Matt. 6:12). Again, He said, "for if you forgive men when they sin against you, your heavenly Father will also forgive you. But if you do not forgive men their sins, your Father will not forgive your sins" (Matt. 6:14–15).

Our debt to God is enormous when compared to others' debts to us. This is illustrated by the vastness of the debt of the unmerciful servant. His debt of millions was beyond comparison to the debt owed to him. We have sinned greatly, and there is no way that we can atone for our sins; but Jesus came and made atonement for them. In a word, humanity's debt to God is so tremendous that we could never pay it. All of my life, I will be indebted to a man who paid my tuition debt for me. He asked nothing in return; but the payment of that debt — it looked so great then — was the difference in my continuing in school or dropping out.

We often expect from others what we are not willing to give. This is true in so many avenues of life. It is easy to see the faults of others but not to recognize our own. Most of us expect our fellow-human beings to forgive us when we make mistakes or sin against them; but often we may not be willing to forgive others. I have known people who have held an unforgiving spirit against a brother or sister for many years. Remember this: the one who is not willing to forgive others is hurt far more than the unforgiven person.

Surely the most significant lesson that Jesus gave in this parable is His final statement: "This is how my heavenly Father will treat each of you unless you forgive your brother from your heart" (v. 35).

"Learning to Live" from this Parable

Lightfoot reminds us that "this parable is striking and impressive because of its acute contrasts. First, there is the contrast of Peter's number and the Lord's. . . . Second, there is the contrast of the two debts. . . . Third, there is the contrast of the creditors. The mighty king forgave, but the lowly servant would not."[4] There are several lessons that we can learn and put into practice in our own lives.

First, *we must learn the "fine art of forgiveness."* It is not easy to learn. Can you imagine the difficulty that Jesus experienced when, as He was hanging on the cross, He said, "Father, forgive them, for they do not know what they are doing" (Luke 23:33)? Forgiveness is truly an art. The more one practices forgiveness, the easier it becomes — in most instances — for one to forgive. When one forgives someone else, the release of that burden is such a relief for the forgiver.

Second, *everyone is indebted to God; thus our willingness to forgive others becomes more imperative.* Each of us is created pure and without sin. He *could* have willed that we be incapable of sin. But instead, He made us capable of sinning so that we could realize the greatness of His gifts to us. Because we are so sinful, we must turn for forgiveness to the one against whom we have sinned. We are "free moral agents." We are not *compelled* to obey God; but when we do submit to Him, we are then "compelled" to live faithfully. This faithfulness includes accepting forgiveness through obedience to Him; and it includes being willing to forgive our brothers and sisters when they sin against us.

Third, *forgiveness is the art of acting as though "it" never happened.* You have often heard that we should "forgive and forget." I am not sure that this is humanly possible. I'm not even sure that God forgets. Scripture says He "will remember no more" (Jer. 31:34). This may be a different idea altogether. But I'm sure we can't forget. Memories of events are stored in our brains and are impossible to totally erase unless we suffer some physical damage to our brain. But we *can* treat the person whom we have forgiven as though the incident never happened. If you cannot associate with someone who has sinned against you or who has disappointed you by his/her being a sinner without replaying that incident in your mind to the extent that your actions and feelings toward that person are hampered or hindered, perhaps you need to take a second look at your forgiveness! Forgiveness is an act of love, and love *"keeps no record of wrong"* (1 Cor. 13:5). God, the Creator of forgiveness, can forgive us no matter how terrible the sin. Let us each strive toward the example God has given as we forgive one another.

Endnotes for Chapter 19

[1] Barclay, *The Gospel of Matthew: The Daily Study Bible Series*, (Philadelphia: Westminster, 1975), Vol. II, p. 193.

[2] Kistemaker, *The Parables of Jesus*, p. 65.

[3] Arndt & Gingrich, *A Greek-English Lexicon*, p. 762f.

[4] Lightfoot, *Lessons from the Parables*, p. 61.

WHAT LIFE'S ALL ABOUT
20

Someone in the crowd said to him, "Teacher, tell my brother to divide the inheritance with me."

Jesus replied, "Man, who appointed me a judge or an arbiter between you?" Then he said to them, "Watch out! Be on your guard against all kinds of greed; a man's life does not consist in the abundance of his possessions."

And he told them this parable: "The ground of a certain rich man produced a good crop. He thought to himself, 'What shall I do? I have no place to store my crops.'

"Then he said, 'This is what I'll do. I will tear down my barns and build bigger ones, and there I will store all my grain and my goods. And I'll say to myself, "You have plenty of good things laid up for many years. Take life easy; eat, drink and be merry."'

"But God said to him, 'You fool! This very night your life will be demanded from you. Then who will get what you have prepared for yourself?'

"This is how it will be with anyone who stores up things for himself but is not rich toward God" (Luke 12:13–21).

When earthquakes come to Southern California where I live, many people look at life from a different perspective. In fact, a succession of major national disasters — fires, floods, earthquakes, hurricanes — cause us to count our blessings in a different way. What really is important? Jesus stated that "a man's life does not consist in the abundance of his possessions." Several times on television interviews, people have expressed that "I have lost everything, but I am still alive."

The search for meaning in life is all too often tied up in worldly possessions.

I remember many years ago in a college class hearing a professor say, "Almost everything you have can be taken away from you; only that which is within you is secure." Our hope in Christ, our faith, the way we manage our lives, how we view what we have are all great determinants of what life is really all about for each of us.

This story of Jesus is certainly one that belongs among the warning and reward parables. The main character learned the importance of making right decisions, but his lesson came too late. This parable is really focused on how we treat worldly possessions as opposed to how we stress the role that God plays in our lives. Commonly referred to as "The Parable of the Rich Fool," this story contains one of the few times that God calls a person a fool. It was on the night his life was taken from him that God said, "You fool!" (Luke 12:20). He was a fool because he had not learned what life is all about. In our country, we can see many evidences of great riches: fine houses, boats, fine cars, and other "trappings" of the rich person. Yet, none of these satisfies. When a person is wealthy, he/she merely wants more! We can never be satisfied with earth's treasures. Only the peace that God gives can provide real contentment. Look at this parable for a different kind of insight on what is really important.

Background Information

A large crowd "of many thousands" had come together to see and hear Jesus. Before addressing the crowd, He turned to his disciples and warned them to *Be on your guard against the yeast of the Pharisees, which is hypocrisy"* (Luke 12:1). The Pharisees were planning an attack on Jesus to see if they could catch Him contradicting Himself in His teachings.

Exactly when He turned and addressed the crowds is not known.

Jesus taught the people about the care that God provides for His children. He told them that God not only has the power to kill both soul and body, but more than that, He loves and cares for His children even as He does the birds of the heavens. In fact, Jesus stressed that "you are worth more than many sparrows" (Luke 12:7).

What it was that prompted a man in the crowd to ask Jesus to "tell my brother to divide the inheritance with me" (v. 13), we do not know. Nor do we know anything from the text about the conflict between the two brothers. The law of Moses did stipulate that a man's possessions would be divided among his sons: the oldest son would receive two shares and each of the other sons would receive one share of the man's possessions. Evidently in this case, one brother — probably the elder brother — was not making the proper division of property with his younger brother. Jesus did not let himself be drawn into the conflict between the brothers. When He lived on earth, He did not directly conflict with man's society. Jesus merely said, "Man, who appointed me a judge or an arbiter between you?" (v. 14.)

This man was not necessarily an evil man. There is nothing in the text that suggests that he was dishonest. He appears to have gotten his goods fairly and honestly. He appears to have been a hard worker. He planned in his business. When he prospered, he looked ahead to know how he could manage his goods. But he had a personal character flaw: he was selfish and self-centered. At least ten or eleven times in this short quotation that Jesus gives from him, the man uses the first person pronoun. He was overly concerned with his own welfare. He does not appear to be touched by the needs of other people.

In a word, he trusted in his riches! When we allow ourselves to be governed by our possessions, we are seriously exposing ourselves to sin, for Paul states that "the love of money is a root of all kinds of evil" (1 Tim. 6:10).

Examining the Text

From the wording of the text, one might wonder if this rich man actually existed. Jesus said, "of a certain rich man (ἀνθρώπου τινός πλουσίου, *anthropou tinos plousiou*)" (v. 16). Few of Jesus' parables are this specific. Whether he actually existed or not does not affect the meaning of the text. But if the man were known to the hearers, it would only have made His story even more believable to those listening.

A phrase that some of Jesus' disciples had trouble with was "the yeast of the Pharisees" (Luke 12:1). "Yeast," or leaven, is a translation of ζύμης, *zumes*. Since yeast is related to the process of souring or fermenting, the Jewish people often considered it as impure. For example, at the Feast of Passover and at other Jewish holy times and places, the bread must be unleavened bread. So the hypocrisy, or souring of a life, was referred to by Jesus as yeast or leaven. Jesus used this expression on other occasions to refer to the hypocrisy of the Pharisees.

After the rich man made his great expansion plans, God called him a fool (ἄφρων, *aphron*, literally "foolish or ignorant"). He was a fool because he was unable to discern what is important. Marshall wrote, "The man who is not rich in regard to God is indeed poor, no matter how big his bank balance. He is, therefore, in the last analysis a fool, a godless and hence a senseless man (cf. 11:40). He has, as he thought, prepared for his own comfort, but he has not prepared for his ultimate destiny."[1] He was not a fool in that he did not possess mental abilities; he was a fool in that he made the wrong kinds of decisions. In other words, he was senseless.

Purpose and Application

The obvious reason why Jesus delivered this parable was to respond to the request of the member of his audience to "Tell my brother to divide the inheritance with me." There are more important things in the world than getting one's share of the inheritance. Jesus could look into the heart of this man and see what his needs were. He warned both him and the others listening to Him, "Watch out! Be on your guard against all kinds of greed; a man's life does not consist in the abundance of his possessions" (Luke 14:15). There are some very special applications that this parable suggests.

Life consists of more than merely what we have. A.B. Bruce, in commenting on Luke 12:15, wrote that "If life, true life, meant possessions, then the more the better, but it means something far higher."[2] A casual look at the world around us will tell us that wealth in and of itself does not make people happy. Life can be terribly empty and frustrating even though one has far more than his fair share of the world's wealth. Marshall wrote that

> The real life of a man is not dependent on the abundance (περισ–
> σεύω, *perisseuo*, 9:17), or perhaps superfluity . . . of his posses-
> sions; hence avarice is dangerous, since it leads a person to direct
> his aim to the wrong things in life and to ignore what really
> matters, namely being rich towards God."[3]

Some of the happiest people I have known have been those who have very little of this world's goods. But their lives were in spiritual order; they had learned what the important things in life are. This is the thrust of what Jesus is saying.

The rich man stored his riches in the wrong place. Don't misunderstand: Jesus never told us that it is wrong for us to have worldly possessions. But He did tell us where our real riches should be stored. "Do not store up for yourselves treasures on earth, where moth and rust destroy, and where thieves break in and steal. But store up for yourselves treasures in heaven, where moth and rust do not destroy, and where thieves do not break in and steal. For where your treasure is, there your heart will be also" (Matt. 6:19–21). This lesson was taught by Jesus in so many ways: to the teacher of the law wanting to follow Him (see Matt. 8:18–22); in the parables of the Hidden Treasure and the Pearl of Great Price (Matt. 13:44–46); to the rich young ruler (Mark 10:17–31); and in many other situations. The wrong in being wealthy is not the possession of the riches; but, it is what these riches can do to us. They can turn our eyes off of Jesus and cause us to emphasize our possessions more than we do Him. We cannot serve both the gods of mammon (or possessions) and God at the same time. The barns of the rich man of our parable were not the important thing. The man needed to put his wealth in proper focus. Since he did not do this, God called him a "fool."

In this man's planning, He left God out. Now, he may have considered himself a good and righteous man. He may have attended the synagogue regularly; he may have even given of his possessions. But the self-centeredness depicted in this parable leads us to believe that whatever religion he had did not take primary place in his life. Although not specifically stated in the parable, we read between the lines that he may have forgotten the needs of others as he planned for his own increasing wealth. Many years ago, I heard about a man who had a sign on his office wall which read, *"I Am Third."* When asked what that meant, he said, "God is first, my fellowman is second, and I am third." This is the order in which Jesus wants us to arrange our lives.

This is a powerful parable! Jesus may be speaking more

succinctly to most all of us than He has in many of His other teachings. He knows our tendency to go after material possessions. So He warns us about keeping the right focus on them. Although the parable does not say this in so many words, a final application of this parable is, *We cannot take our possessions with us.* Someone has aptly said, "There are no pockets in a shroud." We cannot take our worldly wealth with us; only that which is eternal can be captured in the next world.

"Learning to Live" from this Parable

The title of this chapter is "What Life's All About." What has Jesus said here that you can put into practice in your daily life? Four lessons of life seem to jump out at us as we read this great parable.

First, *In our search for happiness and success, we often look in the wrong places.* This man evidently looked to his possessions, and he did not find lasting happiness and success. We may look at our jobs, our families, our possessions, or our hobbies. All of these may be very important to our well-being; but they are not lasting happiness and success. I have known people who actually allowed their children and family to become excuses for not serving God. Jesus evidently knew this would be the case, so he spoke this shocking challenge:

> When Jesus saw a crowd around him, he gave orders to cross to the other side of the lake. Then a teacher of the law came to him and said, "Teacher, I will follow you wherever you go."
>
> Jesus replied, "Foxes have holes and birds of the air have nests, but the Son of Man has no place to lay his head."
>
> "Another man, one of his disciples, said to him, "Lord, first let me go and bury my father."
>
> But Jesus told him, "Follow me, and let the dead bury their own dead" (Matt. 8:18–22).

In this scenario, Jesus told a man that he shouldn't even go back to bury his father. Many have conjectured what Jesus meant; but the meaning is pretty clear: *nothing* should come between a person and that person's service to Christ. Real happiness and success must be sought after in the right place — *in* Christ Jesus.

In the midst of successful ongoing life, death often seems far away from us. How many of us know people who have died — according to our calculation — long before their time. My own son died very unexpectedly at the age of 32. Dear friends have preceded me in death, and we are made to ask, "Why?" Life from our perspective has no guaranteed timetable. From the realm of God's existence, all can be seen as though it were the present. But from our own view of life, it is quite tenuous. James correctly stated it when he wrote, "Why, you do not even know what will happen tomorrow. What is your life? You are a mist that appears for a little while and then vanishes" (James 5:14). We should constantly live our lives as though this were the last minute we have to live!

Though Jesus did not directly interfere with the culture in which He lived, His way of life altered lives then and will alter lives for good in any culture. If He had wanted to, Jesus could have intervened for this younger brother and could have forced the older brother to divide the inheritance. He had enough power to do that! But Jesus did not interfere with their affairs. They were to follow the normal channels of their time. No, Jesus did not *directly* interfere. But if the principles that Christ outlined are put into practice, cultures will be changed. Jesus did not directly teach against slavery, yet when Jesus' principles are practiced, slavery will cease to be. Jesus did not directly interfere with the way His culture treated women. He did treat them with greater dignity than his fellows did; but Jesus did not directly change many of the unfair cultural practices. Yet, in every culture where Christ rules supreme, the station of womanhood has risen. Granted, there are many people professing to be Christians who do not practice the principles Christ promoted; yet, if we do practice them, many of the things around us will change.

We should not spend our lives working for what may cause hatred and division after we are gone. God addressed this when He pronounced the punishment on the Rich Fool. He said, "You fool! This very night your life will be demanded from you. Then who will get what you have prepared for yourself?" (Luke 12:20). I like the way Lightfoot concludes his discussion of this parable.

> In the height of his prosperity and self-satisfaction, God appeared to the rich man and required his life. How much did he leave? *All that he had.* How foolish that he spent all his life striving for the things he had to leave behind and neglecting the true values that he could have taken with him. He had a good title on earth, and no permanent lease and no title in heaven. One night his soul slipped out from it all — all his wealth and ease and self-indulgence — and went as a hungry beggar into the presence of God. "So is he who lays up treasure for himself, and is not rich toward God."[4]

Too many of us place too great an emphasis on what we have and what we will have left when we leave this world. What we have amassed in the form of possessions does not matter in the eyes of God. How we have used what we have and how we have treated others does matter. But, much greater than this, what we have reserved for God is what really counts.

Endnotes for Chapter 20

[1] Marshall, *Commentary on Luke*, p. 521.

[2] A.B. Bruce, *"The Synoptic Gospels,"* p. 557.

[3] Marshall, *Commentary on Luke*, p. 523.

[4] Lightfoot, *Lessons from the Parables*, p. 81.

THE PERIL OF FRUITLESSNESS
21

The Parable of the Barren Fig Tree: Luke 13:1-9

Now there were some present at that time who told Jesus about the Galileans whose blood Pilate had mixed with their sacrifices. Jesus answered, "Do you think that these Galileans were worse sinners than all the other Galileans because they suffered this way? I tell you, no! But unless you repent, you too will all perish. Or those eighteen who died when the tower in Siloam fell on them — do you think they were more guilty than all the others living in Jerusalem? I tell you, no! But unless you repent, you too will all perish."

Then he told them this parable: "A man had a fig tree, planted in his vineyard, and he went to look for fruit on it, but did not find any. So he said to the man who took care of the vineyard, 'For three years now I've been coming to look for fruit on this fig tree and haven't found any. Cut it down! Why should it use up the soil?'

" 'Sir,' the man replied, 'leave it alone for one more year, and I'll dig around it and fertilize it. If it bears fruit next year, fine! If not, then cut it down' " (Luke 13:1-9).

This parable certainly belongs with the "Warning and Reward" parables. The fig tree, in one sense, represents all of us in that God expects us to be fruitful in our lives. But in order for us to fully appreciate the warning aspect of this parable, we need to look at the situation in which it was given.

Several events had happened since the incident involving the Rich Fool (Luke 12:13-21).

It would appear that the same "crowd of many thousands" (12:1) was still with Jesus, and Luke seems to be indicating that several other incidents took place at or near the same time. The disciples were admonished not to worry about the uncertainty of life, for God is in control and He will care for us (Luke 12:22–34). Then, they were told to be prepared for the return of the master, referring to Jesus' own return (Luke 12:35–48), but His disciples probably did not comprehend the meaning of the message. They were unwilling to accept the idea that He would ever leave them. Then, He warned the disciples that their life of service for Him would not always be a peaceful one; for His coming brought about dissension in families and other very important relationships (Luke 12:49–53), and they needed to be able to read the signs of the times in which they were living. It is in this context that the Parable of the Barren Fig Tree was given to them. But, more about this in the next section.

Background Information

This parable is reported only by Luke, but there are references to fig trees in a number of places in the gospel accounts. The fig tree was a very familiar sight, and since there were many of them, this provided a great opportunity for Jesus' teaching. Barclay has this insightful statement about the fig tree.

> The fig tree was the most valuable of all trees. It was naturally very productive and bore three crops within the year. It was in fact normally in fruit for ten months in the year, April and May being the only two months when figs were not to be found upon its branches. For this very reason it was common to find fig trees planted among the vines. The fig trees were much more certain than the vines and were a stand-by should the vines fail. Normally a fig tree did not fruit for the first three years. The point of the parable is that the master waited the requisite three years for the tree to fruit; at the end of that period it was still unproductive and so he wished to cut it down. But the vine dresser pleads for another chance which would be the last chance of all.[1]

Fig trees were also helpful in that hot, arid part of the world in that its dense foliage provided much needed shade, and this was often thought of symbolically as the shade which God provides for us. It was also a symbol of peace and prosperity (see 1 Kings 4:25). Fig trees were often used as symbols for God's people, both in the Old Testament and the New Testament. So, it is not surprising that Jesus would use the fig tree similarly.

The immediate cause of Jesus' delivering this parable seems to be the news of a calamity that had occurred in Jerusalem. Marshall suggests that "the impression is that messengers have arrived from Jerusalem bringing news of the latest incident there,"[2] namely, the "Galileans whose blood Pilate had mixed with their sacrifices" (Luke 13:1ff) and the incident Jesus mentioned that occurred at the tower of Siloam. Neither of these two events is specifically referred to in any extant history of the times; however, we may assume that the events really did occur since there was not then nor has there since been a strong argument made for their not having occurred.

It is significant also that the people confronted Jesus with the news of this incident of the Galileans. It seems that Jesus Himself may have added the other incident about "the eighteen who died when the tower of Siloam fell on them" (v. 4). The Jewish people believed that sin caused sickness, disease, and painful death. This is discussed in Ezekiel 18:1ff. where the prophet proclaims that it is the soul that sins who will die. But in that passage, Ezekiel was discussing the influence of sin on an individual person's guilt. During Jesus' day, people believed that, when misfortune befalls someone, it is because of some sin they or their parents have committed. In John 9:1ff., Jesus healed a man born blind, and even His disciples asked if the man was born blind because of some sin he or his parents may have committed (v. 2). But Jesus asserted that it was not necessarily because of sin committed. In the text in Luke, Jesus is dealing with this same question. Were the Galileans killed because of their sin? Were the people at the tower of Siloam killed because of their transgressions? Jesus points the question back to the audience and tells them that unless they repent, they may be more sinful than either group mentioned. Marshall comments,

> The report of a tragedy in Jerusalem, thought by Jesus' hearers to be due to the especial sinfulness of those who had suffered in it, leads him to affirm that all of his hearers are equally in danger of divine judgment and to quote a further example from which the same point is repeated. This leads up to a parable indicating that, if Israel does not take the chance of repentance afforded by God's patience, the day of reckoning will duly arrive.[3]

Explaining the Text

As was mentioned earlier, these two illustrations discussed by Jesus are not found in extrabiblical sources. Some critics of the Bible have argued, therefore, that this is proof that the Bible contains unreliable accounts. It proves no such thing. Not all events of history make the history books; but some events or facts that have been denied because they have not been found in extrabiblical sources have embarrassed the critics. One specific instance concerned the Hittites, a group of people mentioned in the Old Testament. These people were not found in extrabiblical sources and so the critics had a "field day" with this. But think of their red faces when the Hittites were found mentioned in some significant archaeological discoveries a few years ago.

The man in our parable had a fig tree planted "in his vineyard" (Luke 12:6). Does it seem strange that a fig tree would be planted in a vineyard? It should not, for often the people of that area planted "fruit gardens" in which there would be different kinds of fruit as well as vineyards. Not only did this conserve space for small areas of tillable ground, but it also served as "insurance" in the event that one or the other did not bear fruit. So, there is nothing strange or unusual about this kind of planting.

In describing the people at Galilee and the victims at the tower at Siloam, Jesus used the word ὀφειλεταί, *opheiletai* (from ὀφείλω, *opheilo*), which means to be indebted. Why Luke used this word for sin rather than some synonym is puzzling. Some suggest that this is to connect the thought of these verses with that of Luke 12:59, "I tell you, you will not get out until you have paid the last penny." At any rate, the guilt of the sin is not affected by the use of this word instead of some word like ἁμαρτία, *hamartia*, to sin or miss the mark.

Jesus described the owner of the fig tree as saying to the vinedresser, ". . . Why should it use up the soil?" (Luke 13:7). The verb used here, and its object, are τήν γῆν καταργεῖ, *ten gen katargei*. It literally means "render the ground useless." It could do this in two ways: first, the fruitless fig tree uses up nutrients in the ground that other plants could use; and second, it takes up space that could be more valuably used for other plants. Is not the same thing true of us if we are "fruitless" in the kingdom? We use up energy that could be spent on others who are more valuable to the kingdom; and we are taking up space that could be more appropriately used by someone who is serious about serving God. The term can also mean to "make of no effect" and it is used by Paul many times to mean "make void, destroy, lose, bring to nought, fail, vanish away," etc. Three places where Paul uses a form of this word to signify "to make of no effect" are Rom. 3:3,31; and Gal. 3:17.

CHAPTER TWENTY-ONE

Purpose and Application

The owner asked that the fig tree be cut down because it was useless. Trees are often cut down for a number of reasons. First, they are cut down because they do not fulfil their purpose. The purpose of the fig tree was to bear fruit, and it did not bear fruit. If it was there to provide shade and it provided shade, then it fulfilled its purpose whether it bore fruit or not. But this tree did not fulfill its intended mission. Second, trees are cut down because they are needed for their "product," usually lumber. Drive through the great Northwest region of our country, and you will see thousands of trees being prepared for making lumber. These trees are not cut down because they do not provide shade; they are cut down because their product — lumber — is perceived to be needed by those removing them. Third, trees are often cut down because they take up space needed for something else — perhaps a house, a shopping center, a field for tillable crops. In some parts of our country — some cities in southern California, for example — special permission has to be received before a tree is cut down. Those who need the space used by the tree have to justify their taking the tree away. In the case of the tree in this parable, the master wanted it out of the way of a more productive tree or vine.

The owner wanted the tree removed because it hindered the land from being productive. "Why should it use up the soil?" he asked. As we have indicated in the previous discussion of the text, the tree sapped the ground of nutrients that could be used for other plants. Often, inactive Christians do more harm than they do good. In the first place, they often occupy the time of church leaders and deprive others of the needed attention that the shepherds would provide to the hurting and hungry. In the second place, they are often a reflection on the church because the non-believers often look to them as examples of what Christians should be. Have you ever heard the excuse, "I don't go to church because of the hypocrites there"? Well, this is a lame excuse; but inactive or hypocritical Christians give these people an excuse to use. We should not allow inactivity or unfruitfulness of Christians to sap the very energy out of the church. The owner in this parable, as well as his vinedresser, were disappointed with the tree because it had not done what it should.

The master's patience was worn out. He had waited the expected three years for the tree to become productive; it had not. He wanted the tree removed. God can grow tired of our continual uselessness. Look at the history of Israel in the Old Testament. How many times did God almost give up on His people. Do you recall Moses' begging God to have mercy on His people when God was ready to give up on them?

Yet, in spite of all of this, God is merciful to us and will give us another chance. The vinedresser pled with his master to give him one more year to dig around the tree and fertilize it. If it did not then bear fruit, he would cut it down. It is interesting to note that Jesus does not give us the master's response to his vinedresser. I think we can safely assume, knowing the longsuffering of God, that the tree was given another year. We know for certain that God is "patient with [us], not wanting anyone to perish, but everyone to come to repentance" (2 Pet. 3:9).

"Learning to Live" from this Parable

When one looks at the illustrations of the Galileans and the victims at the tower of Siloam, there may be a little difficulty in identifying the full purpose that Jesus had for this parable. However, Jesus is certainly wanting us to see the importance of faithfulness and fruitfulness. How much stronger the church would be if we could only learn the lessons of this parable!

In addition to the lessons noted above, how can we further apply this parable to our own daily lives?

We should remember that even God's chosen can become useless. All of us know that when we do not use our physical bodies or parts of our physical bodies, they tend to atrophy. Have you ever injured your leg and had to stay off of it for a period of time? You recall that when you were allowed to begin walking again, you had trouble doing so. The principle is the same in spiritual life. If we do not use our spiritual talents, we tend to lose them. Even though we are "God's chosen," it is necessary for us to put effort in exercising the gifts we have. We can become useless, just as this tree was useless. We can lose our spiritual strength if we are not actively seeking to follow Christ.

We can be lost even though we are AMONG other Christians. It is much easier for us to be faithful to God when we are associating with those who believe and act as we do. But even in this kind of a relationship, we can still become useless. Over the scope of my life, I have known many Christians who were faithfully carrying out the "letter of the law" of Christ; yet they withered inside and became useless. Sometimes trees have to be removed from among other trees of their own kind; and sometimes Christians who are not functioning properly have to be removed from among other Christians. The Corinthian church, for example, was told by Paul to separate themselves from the immoral man among them (see 1 Cor. 5:1–11). Not only should those who are doing wrong be warned of their wrongdoing, but constant association with those not functioning as God wants them to will influence the faithful.

But again, *more patience and understanding needs to be extended to the spiritually weak; they might bear fruit if we will continue to work with them.* Just as the vinedresser wanted the tree to be given another chance, so God wants His weak, struggling children to be given another chance. He is patient and does not want any to perish. We Christians, from our human perspective, are impatient all too often. One who has been captured by sin finds it difficult to break suddenly and live a Christian life. But God is longsuffering and patient; He is willing for us to have other opportunities to obey Him. Why can't we give others second chances, and even lend a hand to help them overcome their struggles with sin?

Best of all, *we all have a season of fruitfulness.* Each of us has the ability to bear fruit. We may become discouraged when we struggle with Satan. But if we will cultivate and fertilize our lives with the word of God and the exercise of Christian living, we may be given a fertile future in serving God.

Endnotes for Chapter 21

[1] Barclay, *And Jesus Said*, p. 127.

[2] Marshall, *Commentary on Luke*, p. 553.

[3] *Ibid.*, p. 552.

WHAT SHALL WE DO WITH THE SON?
22

The Parable of the Wicked Vinedressers:
Matt. 21:33–46; Mark 12:1–12; Luke 20:9–18

"Listen to another parable: There was a landowner who planted a vineyard. He put a wall around it, dug a winepress in it and built a watchtower. Then he rented the vineyard to some farmers and went away on a journey. When the harvest time approached, he sent his servants to the tenants to collect his fruit.

"The tenants seized his servants; they beat one, killed another, and stoned a third. Then he sent other servants to them, more than the first time, and the tenants treated them the same way. Last of all, he sent his son to them. 'They will respect my son,' he said.

"But when the tenants saw the son, they said to each other, 'This is the heir. Come, let's kill him and take his inheritance.' So they took him and threw him out of the vineyard and killed him.

"Therefore, when the owner of the vineyard comes, what will he do to those tenants?"

"He will bring those wretches to a wretched end," they replied, "and he will rent the vineyard to other tenants, who will give him his share of the crop at harvest time."

Jesus said to them, "Have you never read in the Scriptures:

" 'The stone the builders rejected
has become the capstone;
the Lord has done this
and it is marvelous in our eyes'?

"Therefore I tell you that the kingdom of God will be taken away from you and given to a people who will produce its fruit. He who falls on this stone will be broken to pieces, but he on whom it falls will be crushed."

When the chief priests and the Pharisees heard Jesus' parables,

217

they knew he was talking about them. They looked for a way to arrest him, but they were afraid of the crowd because the people held that he was a prophet (Matt. 21:33–46; see also Mark 12:1–12; Luke 20:9–18).

This parable brought about an immediate response from those who were working for the fall of Jesus. Matthew concludes his report of the parable with the statement, "When the chief priests and the Pharisees heard Jesus' parables, they knew he was talking about them. They looked for a way to arrest him, but they were afraid of the crowd because the people held that he was a prophet" (Matt. 21:45–46). This parable was given in the final week of Jesus' personal ministry, and it is not difficult to perceive that His teachings, as well as the negative attitudes toward Him, are becoming more intense. Thielicke makes a very incisive observation as he begins his discussion of this parable:

> If we were to survey all the parables of Jesus we would note something that is very remarkable. All the parables that deal with nature — the lilies of the field, the birds of the air, the shepherd and his sheep — breathe something of peace and safety and order. But whenever man occupies the center — no matter whether it be the unmerciful servant, the unjust steward, the rich man, or whoever it may be — there is always the element of dramatic tension, conflict, doom, and downfall.[1]

In this parable, Jesus really addresses one of the burning issues of His life: the desire of the religious leaders to destroy Him. As one will observe, there were repeated attempts on the part of the religious leaders and prominent citizens of His day to have Him arrested. We noted earlier that Jesus was a revolutionary, and those who saw Him striking at their comfortable and familiar system became incensed. This parable, as we shall see, is closely tied to the incidents of the immediate context.

218

Background Information

In this final week of Jesus' earthly life there is a flurry of activity, and each day is more hectic and more filled with controversial issues. Two extremely controversial actions of Jesus have taken place. First, He has made His triumphal entry into Jerusalem, riding on a donkey (Matt. 21:1–11). The people who were following Him were greatly impressed and "the whole city [of Jerusalem] was stirred" (Matt. 21:10–11). Second, after the triumphal entry, Jesus went to the temple and saw what He regarded as godless acts of the money-changers. He then cleansed the temple (Matt. 21:12–17). This obviously angered not only the money-changers but also the religious leaders who had allowed this to take place. His authority was questioned, animosity was engendered, and He spoke parables that focused attention on how the Jewish leaders had gone with the crowds and dishonored God.

That Jesus would ride on a donkey into the city in His moment of triumph may seem strange. We often regard donkeys as less honorable animals than horses. However, in Jesus' day, horses were ridden into battle; donkeys were ridden at times of regal honor and circumstance. So, it is highly appropriate for Jesus to have ridden on such an animal.

This parable is found in all Synoptic gospels, and there are very few differences in the report that each gives. The picture that Jesus depicts is a very familiar one. The owner of the land often lived in another city; or perhaps his prominence involved traveling out of the area. Absentee landlords were very common.

This incident described very appropriate pictures of Jesus' day. In fact, as one looks at the criminal climate of our day, it is easy to see strong similarity. Palestine was a very "explosive" place in those days, with much crime. But Jesus was interested in impressing on His listeners the "crime" of their rejecting God. Thielicke observes that it "is the story of a clash between God and man."[2] And so, when Jesus told the story, it is easy to see why the Jewish leaders became incensed enough to want His arrest, for they could see themselves in the picture Jesus had painted. Although this parable has a great likeness to an analogy, one must be careful that the comparison is not taken to the extreme.

Explaining the Text

As noted earlier, this parable is in all three of the synoptic gospels. There is no apparent disagreement or conflicts between the three accounts. The texts, for the most part, are relatively simple and easy to understand.

Matthew is a little more explicit about who the person is who planted the vineyard. Mark and Luke both simply call him "a certain man"; Matthew refers to the "certain man" as οἰκοδεσπότης, *oikodespotes*, "master of the house."[3] The New International Version translates this as "landowner," while the Revised Standard Version translates it as "householder." But later on in the parable in Matthew, we are told who the "certain man was." Jesus asked them, "Therefore when the owner of the vineyard comes. . . " (Matt. 21:40). From this, then, we can conclude that he was undoubtedly the landowner, and the NIV has correctly interpreted the sense of the passage.

Regarding the tenants in the parable, all three of the synoptic writers use the word γεωργούς, *georgous*, "one who tills the soil, a farmer, a vinedresser, tenant farmer."[4] So, in this instance, they are land-workers. They were not seen as slaves who were owned by the master, but they appear to have been men who were knowledgeable about farming and who were hired by the "master of the house."

The language of the text is very accusative of the Jewish nation; for it was a known fact that many of the prophets whom God had sent to the Israelites had been mistreated and some of them killed. Jesus undoubtedly used the "son" in the parable as representing Himself, the personal envoy from God. God had sent prophets and other teachers, but He reserved His own Son as His last emissary. Since Jesus had publicly claimed to be the Son of God, the Jewish leaders had no difficulty in making the application of what Jesus was saying. So they "looked for a way to arrest him" (Matt. 21:46).

Wenham makes two poignant statements about this text. He says that "the general drift of the parable is plain. It is the story of God sending first the prophets and then Jesus to the people of Israel, patiently calling them to 'bear fruit'. It is the story of their violent rejection of that call. . . ."[5] The second statement Wenham makes is, "The parable makes it clear that Jesus sees his own death as the climax of the people's rejection of God's invitation to them to fulfil their proper role, an invitation brought first by the prophets and then by Jesus."[6]

The "stone the builders rejected" is unquestionably referring to Jesus. As a young boy, I remember hearing three very precious aunts of mine tell a very interesting story. They said they had heard that there was a tradition from the days of Solomon's building the temple which involved a very peculiarly shaped stone. Finding no place for it, the builders tossed it aside. But, when the building neared completion, there was a gaping hole for which no stone could be found. Then the "stone which the builders had rejected" was found, and it not only fit perfectly, but it proved to be the "capstone" of the building. I cannot vouch for the accuracy of the story, but I can testify that Jesus is that very stone in God's spiritual building which fits perfectly. Surely this "is marvelous in our eyes" (see Matt. 21:42).

CHAPTER TWENTY-TWO

Purpose and Application

The message of this parable almost makes the landowner or master of the house appear totally defeated. He had sent his servants to collect the fruit, and the tenants had beaten and killed the messengers. He then sent larger numbers of servants and they were treated similarly. Finally, he sends his son, thinking that surely they would respect him. But the tenants killed him also. Imagine the hallowed silence in heaven as God made His choice to send the Christ. He had sent prophets, and they were killed. Now the great announcement is made to the heavenly host that God is sending the closest to Himself to bring the message of salvation. Angels must have hung on to the news with awesome surprise; the heavenly host must have been amazed. But God could do no other, for this is the price of love — to give the best you have for those you love, and God loved us so much that He sent His Son (John 3:16).

The son in the parable points to Jesus who was God's final offering to mankind. The vinedressers had decimated the other representatives that the householder had sent to claim the fruit from his vineyard. The final emissary was his son, whom he thought they would respect. So it was with God. He sent His Son to bring the message of salvation, and the people rejected Him by killing Him on the cross. In the parable, Jesus asked His listeners, "Therefore, when the owner of the vineyard comes, what will he do to those tenants?" (Matt. 21:40). His question was answered in the next verse: "He will bring those wretches to a wretched end . . . ." In the same manner, God will not permit His creatures to mistreat His Son without dire consequence. Holy Scripture warns us against turning our backs on God, or "crucifying" Christ all over again (see Heb. 6:1–6).

The patience of God caused Him to give ample opportu-

nity for repentance, as is illustrated by the three trips taken to collect the fruit. Each trip was thwarted, and the same was true when God sent His prophets over and over again — only to have them rejected. So, when God's Son was sent, it is no surprise that they killed Him. No matter how God treats humanity, it seems that we are prone to turn against Him. Lightfoot has this to say about how we respond to God:

> One lesson of the parable is that human privileges and human responsibilities cannot be taken lightly. When God makes provision for man, He expects something in return. This is the way it has always been. When times are good as they are now, when human freedoms are many, when the opportunities of living in such a great land are so unlimited, God surely expects much of all of us.[7]

This statement should awaken all of us to our responsibilities to God. We cannot afford to reject the Son Who was sent to redeem us. If we do, there will be dire consequences.

"Learning to Live" from this Parable

This parable says something about privilege and responsibility. In attempting to apply this parable to own daily lives, let's look back to the last paragraph. We wonder how God views this great land of ours — America. We certainly are among the most fortunate in the world; yet we, as a whole, seem to give less to see His will fulfilled than poorer nations. Many American churches are dying and others are dwindling to mere skeletons of what they used to be. Is it because people no longer will accept the gospel? Absolutely not! We are just not reaching out to them. We have received salvation as a *privilege*, and it is our *responsibility* to be faithful stewards of what God has given us.

We are free moral agents. We are not forced to obey God. Do you ever wonder why God did not make us like automatons, unable to make our own decisions? Why didn't He make us so that we could not sin? Why all of the decisions that we have to make? Because God wants our obedience to be the result of our love for Him rather than because we have no choice in the matter. God does not force us to obey Him; but we will suffer the consequences if we do not obey Him. It is our choice!

God is patient and longsuffering with us. He has given and will continue to give us many opportunities to obey Him. But eventually His patience will run out. Just as the vinedressers were given many opportunities to respond to the call from the owner to send fruit from His investment, so God gives us many opportunities to bring forth fruits worthy of our repentance. Jesus appropriately responds, "I tell you that the kingdom of God will be taken away from you and given to a people who will produce its fruit" (Matt. 21:43). Look around you, my friend. There are already evidences that the kingdom is being taken from us and being given to another. We have allowed the unbelievers to challenge our faith, and we have not responded. Will the time come when this great nation of ours will not be the missionary nation that sends teachers to other nations, but will become a nation that has to be evangelized by others all anew? You and I hold the answer to that. Do not reject the Son who is being sent to claim the fruit from the vineyard of God!

Endnotes for Chapter 22

[1] Thielicke, p. 104.

[2] *Ibid.*

[3] Arndt & Gingrich, *A Greek-English Lexicon* p. 558.

[4] *Ibid.*, p. 157.

[5] Wenham, *The Parables of Jesus*, p. 127.

[6] *Ibid.*

[7] Lightfoot, *Lessons from the Parables*, p. 162.

THE CLOSED DOOR
23

The Parable of the Ten Virgins: Matt. 25:1–13

"At that time the kingdom of heaven will be like ten virgins who took their lamps and went out to meet the bridegroom. Five of them were foolish and five were wise. The foolish ones took their lamps but did not take any oil with them. The wise, however, took oil in jars along with their lamps. The bridegroom was a long time in coming, and they all became drowsy and fell asleep.

"At midnight the cry rang out: 'Here's the bridegroom! Come out to meet him!'

"Then all the virgins woke up and trimmed their lamps. The foolish ones said to the wise, 'Give us some of your oil; our lamps are going out.'

" 'No,' they replied, 'there may not be enough for both us and you. Instead, go to those who sell oil and buy some for yourselves.'

"But while they were on their way to buy the oil, the bridegroom arrived. The virgins who were ready went in with him to the wedding banquet. And the door was shut.

"Later the others also came. 'Sir! Sir!' they said. 'Open the door for us!'

"But he replied, 'I tell you the truth, I don't know you.'

"Therefore keep watch, because you do not know the day or the hour" (Matt. 25:1–13).

The saddest words that I can imagine are *"And the door was shut!"* In the context of this parable, this is ultimate finality; for when the doors to the marriage were shut, they would be opened to no one. This story, therefore, is an excellent illustration of the "Warning and Reward" parables. If we are not ready when the bridegroom (Jesus) comes, the door will be shut and He will begin the celebration without us. What a tragedy for us to have lived our lives in anticipation of His coming and then to be shut out because insufficient preparations were made.

Marriages usually focus on the bride. She is the centerpiece for the wedding, and all plans are made to insure that her wedding day is a very special occasion. However, in this wedding, it is the bridegroom and, especially, the bridesmaids who are central in the story. Jesus is teaching about the importance of making proper preparations in life, and He uses the illustration of a wedding, with the five foolish bridesmaids and their lack of preparation, as the focal point of His teaching.

Background Information

"No one knows about that day or hour" (Matt. 24:36; see 24:42, 50). What a foreboding thought! All of us want to be able to know what will happen. We predict the weather; we predict the stock markets; we predict our earnings; we predict almost everything. We want to know what will happen. But Jesus, in the chapter preceding our text, makes it clear that the time of the coming of the Son of Man is unknown. The events and teachings of chapter 24 of Matthew are directly related to what comes in chapter 25. Jesus had discussed the destruction of Jerusalem and the coming of the Son of God at the end of this age. Then, in this chapter, He discussed the need for the ten virgins to be prepared when the bridegroom in the parable of the ten virgins came, the need for properly using our talents in the parable of the talents, and the coming judgment of all mankind in the final section of the chapter. This is the context of this parable. Weddings are such special occasions, and wedding feasts are most always very festive

and joyous events. Weddings were especially important in ancient Jewish culture. In this parable, Jesus very correctly depicted what happened at a Jewish wedding. Barclay tells us that there were three stages of the Jewish marriage.

> First, there was *the engagement*. This was usually carried out by the parents or by professional match-makers. At this stage the couple might be mere children and probably would never even have seen each other. . . .
>
> Second, there was *the betrothal*. This happened when the couple were approaching marriageable age. It was carried out with feasting and ceremony almost as elaborate as the marriage itself. It was absolutely binding and could not be broken except by divorce. . . .
>
> One year after that, came *the marriage proper*. It was a time of great joy. Everyone joined in the festival and in the procession to the home of the newly-married couple.[1]

We do not know much about the marriage ceremony itself, but the events leading up to that are pretty clear. Usually the bride would choose ten young maidens. Since the bride would likely be in her mid-teens when she married, her friends, selected to be bridesmaids, would likely also be young virgin teenagers. As the parable indicates, they would proceed to the vicinity of the bride's home to await the coming of the bridegroom as the time of the actual wedding drew very close. One never knew exactly when the bridegroom would come, for it was unannounced until just as he was coming. Perhaps he was detained while settling the dowry; maybe there were other preparations that needed to be completed. So, those in attendance at the wedding would need to make proper preparations for a longer-than-usual wait. In this case, five of the virgins did not bring enough olive oil to put in their lamps to keep them burning, for the oil would need to be replaced every fifteen to thirty minutes. The lamps were probably "made of pottery, shaped like a circular, covered bowl. On the side of each lamp a loop-like handle was affixed; at another point on the side there was a small opening where the wick was placed; and on the top was another opening to receive the oil."[2]

So, the waiting begins. Maybe hours pass before the expected call, "The bridegroom comes!" While the final preparations were being made, the five "foolish" (μωραί, *morai*, literally "dull or stupid") found that their oil was nearly depleted and they tried to borrow from the "wise" or prudent virgins. As was the custom in many middle Eastern cultures, when all had arrived at the wedding, the door was shut and was not opened for anyone else. So, when the foolish virgins returned from buying more oil, the door was closed and, presumably, locked.

Explaining the Text

The way this parable is worded almost tempts the interpreter to view it as an analogy rather than as a parable. Although there are some aspects of the analogy that we can follow, it would be a mistake to interpret it throughout as an analogy (i.e., making each part of the parable stand for something specific). It is perhaps true that the virgins represent Christians and the Bridegroom represents Christ, and that the wedding feast has the eternal celebration of victory of God's people in mind. But the analogy stops here. We must avoid the temptation of making each item fall into such a neat little package.

Why there were "ten" virgins was explained earlier: that just seems to be how many bridesmaids were selected in Jewish weddings. These ten virgins would be dressed in white and would most likely be the special friends of the bride.[3] That these bridesmaids "became drowsy and fell asleep" (ἐνύσταξαν πᾶσαι καί ἐκάθευδον, *enustaxan pasai kai ekatheudon*, "they all dropped off to sleep and went on sleeping") is not a negative. Since they did not know when the bridegroom would arrive, it would be normal for them to sleep if they needed to, so they could perform their duties well when the time came.

"And the door was shut" (καί ἐκλείσθη ἡ θύρα, *kai ekleisthe he thura*) is interpreted by A.T. Robertson as "and the door was shut to stay shut"[4] since the grammatical construction of the verb is an aorist passive indicative form. And, this is certainly the meaning we get from ancient sources regarding the closed door at weddings.

Purpose and Application

It was stated earlier that it would be easy to make an analogy of this parable. However, we would miss the real meaning that Jesus was communicating. This parable is one of those many very vital topics that Jesus discussed during the last week of His personal ministry. As He drew nearer to Jerusalem and the final events of His life, He became more and more urgent in His appeal to the people. Many had spurned His teaching; they were searching for ways to entrap Him so they could arrest Him. But the urgency of His message became more acute. What was the spiritual message of the Parable of the Ten Virgins?

We must all live in a constant state of preparedness for the coming of the Bridegroom. It is obvious that the Bridegroom in the parable represents Jesus. In the previous chapter of Matthew, Jesus repeatedly told the disciples that they could not know the day nor hour of His Second Coming. There was a need, therefore, to live in a state of expectancy. The reason the five virgins were wise was because they went to await the return of the bridegroom fully prepared. They had brought enough oil to light their lamps even though his returning was delayed. The reason why the five other virgins were "foolish" was because they *did not plan ahead* — they did not bring sufficient fuel for their lamps. The final admonition of Jesus was, "Therefore keep watch, because you do not know the day or the hour" (Matt. 25:13). Almost everything in life that is important to us is accomplished most easily when preparation has been made. This is also true in our waiting for the return of Jesus.

Jesus will return to us to take the redeemed home to glory just as surely as He left the earth. We may not know the day nor the hour — even Jesus did not know this — but He *will* return. One of the most powerful statements in Scripture came at the time of the ascension of Jesus. Luke records it in these words:

> After he said this, he was taken up before their very eyes, and a cloud hid him from their sight. They were looking intently up into the sky as he was going, when suddenly two men dressed in white stood beside them. "Men of Galilee," they said, "why do you stand here looking into the sky? This same Jesus, who has been taken up from you into heaven, will come back in the same way you have seen him go into heaven" (Acts 1:9–10).

Waiting for the return of Jesus does not mean to stand looking into the heavens for His return. Throughout history, there have been predictors of the return of Jesus, but none of them has made the correct prediction. Many, upon hearing these predictions, sell their property and just *wait* for the coming of the Lord. This is not what Jesus expects of us. We must be *actively involved* in the Christian life and in evangelizing the world until the moment that He returns.

All who are faithful will "enter in"; all others will be shut out. This chapter is entitled "The Closed Door," and the statement "and the door was shut" contains the saddest possible words we could ever hear. There are no words strong enough to express the urgency of the lessons that Jesus is trying to impress upon us in this parable! When that door is shut, no one can open it! It will be shut forever.

"Learning to Live" from this Parable

Righteousness, goodness, faith, and character are not transferrable. There are some things in life that no one can do for us. You cannot be saved for me. You cannot be a Christian or a child of God for me. Someone has very appropriately said, "God has no grandchildren, only children!" This may sound trite to you, but it is filled with truth. I cannot obey God for my children; my parents could not obey God for me. I have to "work out" my own salvation (see Phil. 2:12–13). There are just some things in life that we simply must pay the price to obtain. I cannot build your character for you; I cannot believe God for you. I cannot be baptized for you, even though some claim that they can. I must obey God *all by myself, all for myself!*

There are some things that we cannot borrow. Barclay has this to say about this parable: "It warns us that there are certain things which cannot be borrowed. The foolish virgins found it impossible to borrow oil, when they discovered they needed it. A man cannot borrow a relationship with God; he must possess it for himself. . . . There are certain things we must win or acquire for ourselves, for we cannot borrow them from others."[5] It is apparent from this parable that not everyone in the church will be saved, because not everyone in the church will be continually prepared for the coming of Christ.

And the door was shut! If there were one lesson that I could burn on your consciousness, dear reader, it would be "Don't let the door shut with you on the outside!" Heaven will be too sweet and Hell will be too long and terrible for us to be unprepared to enter into the banquet hall when the Bridegroom calls us to His feast.

CHAPTER TWENTY-THREE

Endnotes for Chapter 23

[1] Barclay, *And Jesus Said*, p. 133.

[2] Lightfoot, *Lessons from the Parables*, p. 166.

[3] Kistemaker, *The Parables of Jesus*, p. 129. See also footnote 1 in same reference.

[4] A.T. Robertson, *Word Pictures in the New Testament*, (Nashville: Broadman Press, 1930), I, p. 198.

[5] Barclay, *The Gospel of Matthew*, Vol. II, pp. 320–321.

COME WORK IN MY VINEYARD
24

The Parable of the Laborers in the Vineyard: Matt. 20:1–16

"For the kingdom of heaven is like a landowner who went out early in the morning to hire men to work in his vineyard. He agreed to pay them a denarius for the day and sent them into his vineyard.

"About the third hour he went out and saw others standing in the marketplace doing nothing. He told them, 'You also go and work in my vineyard, and I will pay you whatever is right.' So they went.

"He went out again about the sixth hour and the ninth hour and did the same thing. About the eleventh hour he went out and found still others standing around. He asked them, 'Why have you been standing here all day long doing nothing?'

" 'Because no one has hired us,' they answered.

"He said to them, 'You also go and work in my vineyard.'

"When evening came, the owner of the vineyard said to his foreman, 'Call the workers and pay them their wages, beginning with the last ones hired and going on to the first.'

"The workers who were hired about the eleventh hour came and each received a denarius. So when those came who were hired first, they expected to receive more. But each one of them also received a denarius. When they received it, they began to grumble at the landowner. 'These men who were hired last worked only one hour,' they said, 'and you have made them equal to us who have borne the burden of the work and the heat of the day.'

"But he answered one of them, 'Friend, I am not being unfair to you. Didn't you agree to work for a denarius? Take your pay and go. I want to give the man who was hired last the same as I gave you. Don't I have the right to do what I want with my own money? Or are you envious because I am generous?'

"So the last will be first, and the first will be last" (Matt. 20:1–16).

This parable is "sandwiched" between two similar statements found in Matt. 19:30 and Matt. 20:16. And it is a sober reminder that we mortals often get our priorities in the wrong order. That which seems so important to us may be a passing fancy in the great order of things. Many of the laborers in the vineyard of which Jesus spoke had the wrong emphasis on things of this world, and Jesus told them that there were more important elements of our existence that we should be concerned with.

Background Information

This parable very appropriately relates to the surrounding scriptures and the context in which these biblical texts are given. You will note that the parable is recorded only by Matthew. Mark's account of this period of Jesus' life includes some of the same background incidents as does Luke, but neither of them tells of the workers in the vineyard. It appears that a crowd of people were following Jesus, and one of them — a young ruler — had raised a question.

In the nineteenth chapter, Matthew records Jesus' teaching on divorce, His blessing of the little children around Him, and the story of the rich young ruler. The rich young ruler is probably more related to this parable because of Jesus' discussion of the young man's riches. The young ruler had asked how he could have eternal life. Jesus, knowing of his priorities, told him that he must sell what he had and give to the poor. The man left sorrowfully because he had great wealth. Jesus' disciples were amazed at His reply to the young ruler and asked Him "Who then can be saved?" (Matt. 19:20ff.). What of those who had forsaken all for Jesus? It was in response to this that Jesus told them that the first would be last and the last would be first.

Jesus was addressing a very common practice. In fact, in a

number of Southern California towns and suburbs, it is not unusual to see as many as 50-100 migrant workers standing by the side of the road, "waiting to be hired." Throughout the day, people will drive by and select someone from those waiting to do work for them. So, it's not difficult to conceive of this story actually happening.

However, it is a little unusual for a person to come out at five o'clock and hire someone for the same amount as he intends to pay others he has hired earlier in the day. William Taylor states that "this parable is harder to interpret than any other which the Saviour uttered."[1] His problem with it is the eleventh-hour man, from the point of view of hiring someone so late and also paying him the same as all the others. Lightfoot seems to be in agreement with Taylor, for he wrote, "We are confronted here with the most puzzling of all the parables."[2] Of course, it may be a little unusual for all persons to be paid the same amount, as Jesus suggests, but He is obviously doing this for a specific purpose. But that a landowner would come by and hire a worker at the eleventh hour could be rationalized. Taylor mentions that "Josephus indeed tells us that the high priest Annas gave the workmen employed in repairing or adorning the temple a whole day's pay, even though they labored for a single hour. . . ."[3] If he has a task that needs finishing and he does not have sufficient laborers to complete it, then he will certainly hire additional workers to complete the job.

Explaining the Text

The landowner (or, οἰκοδεσπότῃ, *oikodespote*, literally "a house ruler") went out at different hours during the day. The Jewish/Roman day of that time was divided into twelve parts, or hours, usually beginning at six o'clock in the morning. The third hour, therefore, would be about nine o'clock in the morning and so on throughout the day. We have no idea why the landowner went out at several times, but, this does not affect the purpose of Jesus' parable.

The landowner agreed to pay the workers a denarius (δενάριον, *denarion*, about one day's wages, or about 20 cents). Later on, when the payment is made, some of the workers who had worked all the day were jealous that they were paid the same amount — a denarius — that the eleventh hour worker was paid. Jesus' parabolic reponse to this was, "Friend, I am not being unfair to you" (Matt. 20:23). After all, did he not pay each person what he had promised to pay? He said, "Don't I have the right to do what I want with my own money?" (v. 15). Jesus impressed upon the other workers that the landowner should not be criticized for being generous.

Purpose and Application

This parable teaches us that we will be rewarded more for our motive than for our deeds. There is no possible way we could ever expect the great rewards that God will give us based on our paltry deeds. We can, in no way, earn God's favor by what we do. This parable, according to R.C. Trench, "is directed against a wrong spirit of mind, which was notably manifested in the Jews, but which all men in possession of spiritual privileges are here warned against. . . ."[4]

God has the right to reward us however He wishes to; we really have nothing to say in the matter. We lost our birthright through the sin of Adam. God had made humanity clean and pure and without fault. But Adam and Eve fell from God's good favor, and we lost all "bargaining power" with God. Whatever God gives us as our eternal reward will be far more than we could ever imagine or deserve. And, Paul quotes from Isaiah to tell the wonders of God's preparation for us:

"No eye has seen, no ear has heard, no mind has conceived what God has prepared for those who love him but God has revealed it to us by his Spirit" (1 Cor. 2:9–10). Again, Taylor believes that the dealing with a "hireling spirit" — which "is selfish, unamiable, elder-brotherly, surly" whereas the trustful spirit "is humble, contented, happy, choice" — seems to be the main lesson of this parable.[5]

We are rewarded on the basis of how we face opportunity. All of us are faced with many opportunities every day of our lives. Someone has depicted opportunity as a "bald-headed person with only a pig-tail pointing out in front of him." The lesson is that one must grasp opportunity as it comes to you, for after it passes you by there is nothing to take hold of! Opportunity is extremely elusive. One thing that each of the workers in the parable had in common was that they seem to have accepted their very first opportunity to work. We have the opportunity to work for God; God has the right to reward us as He sees fit (see Rom. 9:31ff; 11:22ff).

"Learning to Live" from this Parable

Some may look at this parable and conclude that Jesus is teaching that there are no degrees of reward and punishment in the world to come — all workers will receive the same. Although we do not want to address this subject in this context, it is pretty certain that it is not the purpose of the parable to teach this. Whether there are degrees of reward in the world to come is not the subject of this parable. It is more of an "undeserved favor" concept that seems to be taught here than the kinds of reward we will have. After all, all of us receive an undeserved favor simply by receiving salvation; so when this eleventh-hour man received the same as the other, he was receiving an undeserved favor. Some have suggested that those entering at the eleventh hour (i.e., Gentiles) will be treated with the same mercy as those called earlier (i.e., the Jews) would be treated. This may be too much of an interpretation by analogy, but it is worth thinking about.

It is better to work for what we can give than for what we will receive. This is very unlike a "this-world" viewpoint. Christians are different from people of the world; we have a different agenda than this-world citizens have. Taylor seems to refer to this approach as the "trustful spirit" which was explained a little earlier. The workers should have worked with a trustful spirit rather than with a competitive spirit. Those who work for what they can give receive rewards far greater than those who work solely for what they can get. This is not to say that it is wrong to work for our wages or salary; but if that is *all* we do, we may be very miserable people.

God will treat us right — make no mistake about that. He who would not spare His Son from suffering on our behalf will certainly go the second and third mile — and more — to see that we are treated right. Recall that Jesus quoted the landowner as saying, "I will pay you whatever is right" (Matt. 20:4). We must, however, avoid an envious spirit when we perceive that God is treating others "better" than He is treating us. Such a feeling will fester in our hearts and make us become bitter people. You do the serving; let God do the rewarding! In this way, we relieve ourselves of having to worry about how much better the other person is being treated than we are. The God of all creation knows how to take care of His own.

Take a careful look back at this parable. Why is it that so many have trouble with this parable? Perhaps we all have trouble with it. This parable is about *GRACE*, and grace is of God, not man. We with our "this-world" mindset only know *WAGES*. We don't understand *pure gifts*. The concept of grace is beyond many of us. Maybe one of the most important messages that this parable gives to us is the reality of grace. Neither of the workers in the vineyard deserved to be paid the full price. But the Master treated all of them right. This parable, perhaps more than any other of Jesus' parables, is saying that motive is more important than deeds. If we miss his message, we've missed grace; and if we have missed grace, we've missed salvation. All of the laborers were rewarded for their *willingness* to work, not their work. We don't have to do all that Paul — or anyone else — did; we just have to be *willing to do it.*

Endnotes for Chapter 24

[1] Taylor, *The Parables of Our Saviour*, p. 104.

[2] Lightfoot, *Lessons from the Parables*, p. 147.

[3] *Ibid.*, p. 105.

[4] Trench, *Notes on the Parables*, p. 63.

[5] Taylor, *The Parables of Our Saviour*, p. 112.

AN OFFER WE CAN'T REFUSE
25

The Parable of the Royal Marriage Feast: Matt. 22:1–14

Jesus spoke to them again in parables, saying: "The kingdom of heaven is like a king who prepared a wedding banquet for his son. He sent his servants to those who had been invited to the banquet to tell them to come, but they refused to come.

"Then he sent some more servants and said, 'Tell those who have been invited that I have prepared my dinner: My oxen and fattened cattle have been butchered, and everything is ready. Come to the wedding banquet.'

"But they paid no attention and went off — one to his field, another to his business. The rest seized his servants, mistreated them and killed them. The king was enraged. He sent his army and destroyed those murderers and burned their city.

"Then he said to his servants, 'The wedding banquet is ready, but those I invited did not deserve to come. Go to the street corners and invite to the banquet anyone you find.' So the servants went out into the streets and gathered all the people they could find, both good and bad, and the wedding hall was filled with guests.

"But when the king came in to see the guests, he noticed a man there who was not wearing wedding clothes. 'Friend,' he asked, 'how did you get in here without wedding clothes?' The man was speechless.

"Then the king told the attendants, 'Tie him hand and foot, and throw him outside, into the darkness, where there will be weeping and gnashing of teeth.'

"For many are invited, but few are chosen" (Matt. 22:1–14).

Jesus evidently loved weddings. He used them often in His teaching. In fact, his first miracle was performed while

He was attending a wedding at Cana in Galilee (John 2:1–11). There are several parables and other teachings of Jesus that center around a marriage or some other type of festive occasion.

Background Information

This parable has some problems we should address briefly. In some ways, it sounds like the Parable of Excuses (Luke 14:15–24), often called The Parable of the Great Supper, which we have already studied. But there are enough variations between that one and this one that we are treating them as two different parables. A second problem is explained by Barclay. He wrote, "Verses 1–14 of this chapter form not one parable, but two; and we will grasp their meaning far more easily and far more fully if we take them separately."[1] Barclay believes that the "first" parable involves Matt. 22:1–10 and the "second" parable is in Matt. 22:11–14. He further states in the place cited that verse 7 appears to him to be a statement placed there by Matthew, the author, and it is a reflection of Matthew's experience in the Destruction of Jerusalem; for, this gospel was probably written sometime around 80 A.D. These views expressed by Barclay are not universally held among students of the parables, but they do present an interesting explanation of what is otherwise a difficult parable. For example, the sending of an army and the destruction of the murderers does not sound like the way that Jesus would have handled the situation. But, one must realize that Jesus someday will change roles from that of a savior to that of a judge, and He will indeed mete out judgment to those who reject God. Time, space and the purpose of this study do not merit a lengthy argument of this issue; we will simply attempt to study the parable and learn how we can "learn to live" by what it teaches.

The parable is certainly adapted from Eastern customs. For example, when invitations were sent out, they may or may not have included the actual date or time for the banquet. They would usually be sent out well in advance of the marriage feast. As the time drew nearer and preparations became more specific, a second invitation would be sent, and perhaps a third just prior to the wedding feast. In our own culture, we usually send out one invitation which serves for the wedding as well as the wedding feast (or reception); but, not so for them. So it is not strange that the second invitation would go out to those first invited.

Matthew places this parable directly after the parable of the landowner, in which a man sent his servants and finally his son to collect what was owed, but they were refused and the son was murdered (Matt. 21:33–46). It is generally agreed that both parables address the rejection of the coming of Jesus by the Jews and the inviting of the Gentiles to accept the gospel. There is certainly a parallel between the parable we are now studying and the rejection of Jesus by the Jews and the accepting of Him by the Gentile world. God was saying to the Jewish nation that if they turn their back upon Him, He will offer the message of salvation to others.

Explaining the Text

This is certainly a marriage feast (ἐποίησιν γάμους, *epoiesen gamous*, a wedding feast), as opposed to a wedding, (γάμος, *gamos*, a wedding). Arndt and Gingrich state that the plural (γάμους) was usually used for wedding feasts and the singular (γάμος) was used to signify a wedding ceremony. In fact, they cite Josephus who used the words in this manner.[2] A.B. Bruce explains that the word for wedding feast was plural because marriage feasts lasted for several days, probably seven.[3]

When the king sent out the second invitations, those who were invited "paid no attention and went off. . ." (Matt. 22:5). *"They paid no attention,"* from ἀμελήσαντες, *amelesantes*, a participle literally meaning "being negligent," does not indicate that they were insulting or that they made fun of the invitation. They just did not pay it any attention. They ignored the invitation because they had other things they regarded as more important.

It was bad enough for the people to shun the invitation of the king, but when they took some of the messengers and mistreated and killed them, it was more than the king could take. He became furious and sent his armies out to avenge the death of his servants.

Purpose and Application

The major thrust of this parable was directed against the Jewish nation of Jesus' day and before. As we have seen in other parables, the Israelite people had rejected God's call for mercy through the prophets and now through His own Son. They persecuted, rejected and killed the prophets, and now they are about to kill the Son. Jesus is warning them that the results of their "neglecting" the invitation will be severe.

The universality of God's mercy is seen in the calls the king made to those who were invited. The first invitation was sent to the Jewish nation. Then, the king sent out a follow-up invitation, which demonstrates the depth of God's patience and mercy. When they spurned both the invitations and seized, mistreated and killed the servants, they showed that they were rejecting this mercy. The last invitation in (verses 8 and following) represents God's invitation to the Gentiles: the people on the street corners and "all the people they could find" (vv. 9–10). God had made great preparation for the coming of Christ (see Matt. 22:4; Eph. 1:4; 3:9–11), and He was not going to let the preparation be wasted effort.

God expects those of us who attend the feast to make proper preparation. One man came in "not wearing wedding clothes" (vv. 11–12). When we look at his punishment, we may ask, "isn't this a bit severe?" After all, the king had asked for people from "street corners." But the man could have and should have gone home to change, because the custom of the day was to wear the appropriate attire to a wedding feast. The man was not wearing wedding clothes, so he was excluded. The same will be true when we approach the wedding feast of the Lamb of God. We will be expected to be appropriately attired with the clothing of Christian living and with Christ Himself, and with virtue. God expects us to present a life of holiness to Him; He does not expect perfection, but He *does* expect effort. Paul expresses the nature of the "risen life" very clearly (see Col. 3:1–17).

"Learning to Live" from this Parable

All of us have been invited to the wedding feast of Jesus, the bridegroom of the church. We all have the opportunity to "clothe" ourselves with the appropriate attire for this great feast. We have all experienced the patience and longsuffering of God. He has been merciful with us and has given all of us "second invitations," or second chances.

There are at least four ways of treating God's invitation. First, we can ignore it. This comes as a result of our indifference or neglect. We may have great intentions of doing what is right, but you remember the old saying, "The road to hell is paved with good intentions." Perhaps the people in this parable had, at first, intended to attend, but they neglected to go. Second, we can reject the invitation, even with violence. If we allow our hearts to be filled with malice or prejudice, we will not be open to God's invitation. Third, we can respond with insolence or laziness. How sad it will be when some of us appear in the presence of God and we are not wearing the wedding garment. Oh, we intended to; but we were not willing to put out the effort. Or we thought God was expecting too much from us, so we just decide that we'd show Him: we just wouldn't get ready! Fourth, we can give hearty approval and acceptance to His invitation to His Son's wedding feast.

This parable illustrates to us both the goodness and severity of God. God's goodness is seen in His longsuffering nature and His willingness to give us that second chance — even when all those around us say we won't make it. His severity is seen in the fact that He will punish disobedience. Focus your attention on Romans 11:22: "Consider therefore the kindness and sternness of God: sternness to those who fell, but kindness to you, provided that you continue in his kindness. Otherwise, you will also be cut off."

What a powerful challenge is given to us in this parable! Here in the last days of the earthly life of Christ, He reaches out and challenges us to be prepared when He returns to receive His own. Why not join me and a host of others in planning to be ready when He comes?

Endnotes for Chapter 25

[1] Barclay, *The Gospel of Matthew*, Vol. I, p. 266.

[2] Arndt & Gingrich, *A Greek-English Lexicon*, p. 151.

[3] A.B. Bruce, *The Gospel of Matthew*, in *The Expositor's Greek Testament*, *Vol.* I, p. 269.

A MESSAGE FROM BEYOND
26

The Parable of the Rich Man and Lazarus: Luke 16:19–31

"There was a rich man who was dressed in purple and fine linen and lived in luxury every day. At his gate was laid a beggar named Lazarus, covered with sores and longing to eat what fell from the rich man's table. Even the dogs came and licked his sores.

"The time came when the beggar died and the angels carried him to Abraham's side. The rich man also died and was buried. In hell, where he was in torment, he looked up and saw Abraham far away, with Lazarus by his side. So he called to him, 'Father Abraham, have pity on me and send Lazarus to dip the tip of his finger in water and cool my tongue, because I am in agony in this fire.'

"But Abraham replied, 'Son, remember that in your lifetime you received your good things, while Lazarus received bad things, but now he is comforted here and you are in agony. And besides all this, between us and you a great chasm has been fixed, so that those who want to go from here to you cannot, nor can anyone cross over from there to us.'

"He answered, 'Then I beg you, father, send Lazarus to my father's house, for I have five brothers. Let him warn them, so that they will not also come to this place of torment.'

"Abraham replied, 'They have Moses and the Prophets; let them listen to them.'

" 'No, father Abraham,' he said, 'but if someone from the dead goes to them, they will repent.'

"He said to him, 'If they do not listen to Moses and the Prophets, they will not be convinced even if someone rises from the dead' " (Luke 16:19–31).

This parable has been intentionally placed last for two reasons: first, this is probably my favorite of all of the stories

247

that Jesus told, and second, it brings us face to face with one of the most startling and awe-inspiring scenes that we can imagine. We are given a chance by the Savior to glance for a brief moment into the next world.

This is a very unique parable in several ways. How should it be studied? As a historical event or as a parable? Very early Christian tradition claims that it was a real story.[1] Some of the unique elements of this parable are: first, it is the only parabolic teaching of Jesus that gives such specific information about the characters and events. For example, Jesus says there was a "certain" rich man; He says the poor man's name was Lazarus; and "they have Moses and the Prophets." All of these details, which are lacking in other parables, have caused many to regard these people as real people and the events surrounding their lives as real events. Incidentally, one should not confuse this Lazarus with the Lazarus who was the brother of Mary and Martha, for there is no reason to believe that they are the same. A second unique element is: this story has no introduction or conclusion. It could have been told anytime in the personal ministry of Jesus, but it certainly seems to be more fitting here. Third, there is little question about the purpose and meaning of the story. Although most of us may have our own theories about the source of the story, it does not merit any further discussion for this study. The story teaches the same lessons whether it is real or fictional.

Some religious people claim that when one dies, his/her soul "sleeps" until the resurrection and is not conscious. When this story is used to show otherwise, they claim that the characters in this do not prove otherwise for, after all, they claim, it is *only a parable.* Let us recall that Jesus never misrepresented facts in His parables; so He must be affirming that there is consciousness in the afterlife, and there is feeling of bliss or agony being experienced.

Background Information

Taylor believes that this parable is an extension of, or at least a complement of, Luke 16:8–10. It is true that Jesus, according to Luke, had just spoken the Parable of the Shrewd Manager, and there is certainly a contextual relationship that exists between this parable and the previous one. However, I would prefer to say that this parable is prefaced by the expression "the Pharisees, who loved money, heard all this and were sneering at Jesus" (Luke 16:14*).* This is a more logical connection because Jesus sets forth the story of the rich man and Lazarus to show the futility of riches. The rich man of the parable is a prime example of how riches can destroy our understanding of what is important. Here is an example of how riches can really lead us to become self-centered and uncaring for others, if we aren't very careful.

This parable is a parable of contrasts. Note the following: first, a rich man is lavishing in wealth; a poor beggar is covered with sores and would have been blessed just to have the crumbs from the rich man's table. Second, the rich man "died and was buried"; the poor man just died. We could assume from this that the rich man had all of the pomp surrounding the funeral of a well-to-do person; the poor man may have had no funeral and may have been buried in a potters' field where paupers were buried. Third, the rich man went to Hell (ᾅδης, *hades*); Lazarus, the beggar, was carried to Abraham's bosom (κόλπον, *kolpon*). See the next section for a discussion of both of these terms. Fourth, the attitudes of the two men in the "next" world are a great contrast.

It does seem, however, that these two men were both Jewish men, "sons of Abraham." And, it is not said that one of them was "better" than the other one in a moral sense. The only moral flaw that we might discern is how the rich man regarded the beggar as less than he was, and thus neglected to help him.

This story is a difficult one in some respects. Taylor wrote that "Probably no one of the Saviour's parables needs to be so cautiously handled as this of the rich man and Lazarus."[2] It has not been the purpose of this volume to become a critical work, so we will leave these problems for others. Our purpose is to demonstrate how we can learn to live from these stories that Jesus told.

Explaining the Text

Barclay gave us a most interesting statement when he wrote, "This is a parable constructed with such masterly skill that not one phrase is wasted."[3] Boice wrote that "In all the Bible I do not believe there is a story more stirring or more disturbing than that of the rich man and Lazarus."[4] It is a story that has captured my own lifelong attention, for it seems so real and so certain in the reward and punishment that humanity will experience as a result of how we live on earth. There are several words in this parable that we should briefly discuss.

"There was a rich man" (Luke 16:19, NIV) is literally "A certain man was rich" (ἄνθρωπος δέ τις ἦν πλούσιος, *anthropos de tis en plousios*). Jesus was very specific in describing this man, who was clothed in purple and fine linen, the clothing of royalty. He is often referred to as "Dives" from the Latin word meaning "rich," but no name is given to him in the New Testament.

Then there was also a beggar named Lazarus (Λάζαρος, *Lazaros*, probably a Greek form of the Hebrew word אלעזר, *eleazar*, meaning "God is my help"). Nowhere in all of the parables is Jesus so specific as in this parable, which has caused some students of the parables to believe that this is a true story that Jesus knew from the next world.

The poor man was "covered with sores" (ἡλκωμένος, *helkomenos*, literally "being full of sores"), and it appears that he needed to be carried to the rich man's gate. He didn't ask for much: he only wanted the crumbs that fell from the rich man's table. Some suggest that knives and forks were not used, and hence people ate with their hands, wiping their hands with pieces of bread and throwing it down for the dogs. It may have been this that the poor man wanted — only the crumbs, only the pieces of bread used by the rich man to wipe his hands.

Another contrast involves their position after their death. The rich man was "in hell" (NIV), or ᾅδη, *hade*, literally "hades." Hades was the "realm of the dead." Since death seals our eternal condition, he was actually in pain. The word for "hell," the eternal place of punishment, is γέεννα, *gehenna*. But Lazarus was transported to Abraham's side, or to his "bosom" (κόλποις, *kolpois*, "bosom, breast, chest"[5]). The Scripture does not specifically define what is meant by "Abraham's bosom," but the context suggests that it was a place of comfort and peace — perhaps the waiting place in hades for righteous souls until the final judgment.

Purpose and Application

Kistemaker wrote that "The parable of the rich man and Lazarus may be viewed as a drama in two acts followed by a conclusion. The first scene is a presentation of life and death on earth, and the second portrays heaven and hell. The conclusion is given in the form of implicit application."[6] It is concerned with the certainty of death and of the actuality of reward and punishment.

It does not matter how much you have, but how you use it. This theme is taught in so many of Jesus' parables. A man's

251

life "does not consist in the abundance of what he has," Jesus taught. Taylor wrote, "Not what a man has, but what a man is, counts before God," and "Riches test character in one way, poverty tests it in another."[7] Not all of us will be wealthy, nor will all of us be poor. But, God takes us *as we are* in the midst of what we have. Our eternal reward really depends upon how we have used what we have to become what we are.

Death permanently determines our eternal destiny. Abraham was very explicit when he answered the rich man's request to send Lazarus to dip his finger in water and put it on his tongue: "A great chasm has been fixed" (Luke 16:26). There is no way that one can go from one eternal "place" to another. So, the call to repentance must be answered before it is too late. There is no time for us to waste in making our decision about God — and *we will* make a decision. It may not be the right one, but we will decide to either accept or reject Jesus Christ.

"Learning to Live" from this Parable

Kistemaker states that "the lesson Jesus taught is timeless; it is the abiding rule of listening to God's Word obediently and thankfully."[8] When one reads this parable, an ominous note of warning stands out. As is so often the case, this rich man evidently had no warning that his earthly life was to be taken from him. He was living for the present, and living it to the fullest of his capacity. This is so true of many of us: we live as though we know there will be many more tomorrows; yet, we know not what hour will be our last.

Taylor suggests three lessons that seem appropriate here. First, *the sin of the rich man.* It was not that he was rich, not that he had wasted his wealth, not, to our knowledge, that he had gotten his gain by misusing others. It does not appear that

252

he was a murderer or an adulterer or any other type of blatant sinner. His sin seems to be that "he failed to employ them [his riches] as God's trustee, for the benefit of his fellow-men, and for the glory of Him to whom, of right, they belonged."[9] Second, *"the inexcusableness of this rich man."*[10] If only he could have known what he was doing. How often we cry out, "If I had only known." We cannot blame ignorance for our failure to obey. We cannot blame God nor others for our failures. We can only blame ourselves for our own perversity. Third, *the rich man's punishment.* His punishment was painful and eternal. Taylor states that "we must beware of supposing that in the future life things will be literally as they are here described. I do not believe that it is possible, in our present speech, to portray exactly what the state will be."[11] We as human beings cannot imagine what the spiritual punishment of hell is like. *But it is real!* Why do we no longer warn our fellow-human beings that there is a hell? There is a blatant denial of it. Many people believe that there is a rewarding life after this one, but a large percentage of people do not believe there is a hell. This parable teaches us that there is.

This story suggests that there will be a recognition of persons and states of being in the next life. I must hasten to state that the story does not argue this point; but it does suggest it. The rich man recognized Lazarus; Abraham recognized the rich man. The rich man remembered Moses and the prophets. He remembered his brothers back on earth and wanted someone to be an emissary of salvation to them.

This story also suggests that any kind of "universalism," purgatorial cleansing, or second chance is ruled out. There was a great chasm fixed between the two places of existence. It was not possible for one to cross from one place to the other.

Before I close this chapter, I want to make some personal observations that relate to this great parable. Lots of books, television programs, and other reports of "experiences" relating to the "afterlife" are available today. Everyone seems to be fascinated with the discussion of the afterlife. Some claim to have experienced the "white tunnel" and others report other kinds of experiences. But here in this parable, we have a real look at the afterlife by one Who really knows: Jesus. He gives us a clear and detailed view of the next world. Whether He meant it to be symbolic (like the book of Revelation) or real, we do not know. But what He said IS true. It is real.

Heritage meant a lot to the Jewish people. Hence the image of "Abraham's bosom" was a very meaningful expression. Someone has described our generation as a "cut-flower culture." It is pretty while it lasts, but it soon withers. We often do not give much attention to heritage; but, Lazarus "slept with the fathers." This statement is often used in the Old Testament.

Love is honest, but sometimes very tough. This parable honestly reveals to us the fate of those who neglect God. It is not pretty; it is not desirable. How many of us would have envied the position of Lazarus? Yet, in the long run, his relationship with God was the one most chosen. Appearances can be so deceptive. We observe someone who is wealthy, or who seems to have everything. Yet, often those lives are the most empty of all.

Finally, God will not send a special vision from the world of the dead. We must accept the message that God has given us through His Son, Jesus Christ. As we close this volume, my earnest prayer for you as you read these words is that you will be aware of the certainty of judgment, the beauty of God's love and care for us, and the glory that will be ours when we have finished serving the Lord with all of our heart. We need to learn to live from the message that Jesus has brought to the world. Only by putting His words into our life can they effectually change our lives. My closing prayer is for all men to hear God's message of hope and obey it.

Endnotes for Chapter 26

[1] George A. Buttrick, *The Parables of Jesus* (Grand Rapids: Baker, 1973), pp. 137ff. tells that authors as early as Ambrose and Tertullian [in the third century A.D.] considered it a real story; however he himself believes that it is a parable and should be studied as such. Probably the bulk of Christian scholarship would agree that it is a parable; but, there are still many who would regard it as real. It really makes no difference in the meaning of the parable, for Jesus never misrepresented facts in parabolic teaching.

[2] Taylor, *The Parables of Our Saviour*, p. 387.

[3] Barclay, *Commentary on Luke*, p. 213.

[4] James Montgomery Boice, *The Parables of Jesus* (Chicago: Moody Press, 1983), p. 210.

[5] Arndt & Gingrich, *A Greek-English Lexicon*, p. 442.

[6] Kistemaker, *The Parables of Jesus*, p. 236.

[7] Taylor, *The Parables of Our Saviour*, p. 394.

[8] Kistemaker, *The Parables of Jesus*, p. 245.

[9] Taylor, *The Parables of Our Saviour*, p. 395.

[10] *Ibid.*, p. 397.

[11] *Ibid.*, p. 399.

CONCLUSION TO PART IV: LIFE AND LAST THINGS

Much of today's world is not concerned about "last things." Many are so confident of their position in this world that they will not allow themselves to think about what happens when all is over here. I asked a friend one time, "Do you believe in life after death?" He replied, "I never think about it." He was not being disrespectful; he just honestly had not thought about it. The parables we have just studied have a common thread of meaning running through them: all of us will be accountable for how we have lived.

Forgiveness has such a tremendous place in the life of the Christian. Not only must we accept the forgiveness of God; we must also learn to forgive others. I have referred to "The Fine Art of Forgiveness." It is an art; and the more we practice it, the better we become. Jesus was the model of forgiveness. Can you imagine how difficult it must have been for Him, while hanging on the cross, to cry out to God, "Father, forgive them for they do not know what they are doing"? Yet, is there any doubt in our minds that Jesus truly forgave them?

Life gets tedious, especially when we do not understand it. So often our priorities are improperly placed, and we lose the meaning of what life is really all about. The rich man had directed his entire life to amassing wealth. He did not necessarily mistreat Lazarus; but he did neglect him. He failed to see the real meaning of life. How terribly sad it will be to stand and face the Creator and have Him say, "You just didn't know what you were doing." How sad for us not to bear fruit

257

in all we do. God has, throughout history, called on humanity to obey Him; but we have neglected Him. We have sometimes, as one parable in this group teaches, actually mistreated those who teach God's message and frequently God's messengers have been killed for their beliefs.

We must be prepared when the Master comes. He will come at such a time that some of us will not be ready for Him. As the foolish virgins, many of us will not have enough "oil" to keep our "lights" shining. But, God still calls on us to obey Him. He will treat all of us fairly. One great message threads through the parables: the grace of God. Often, we have neglected to stress the power and freedom of the grace of God. Much of my earlier life in the church, I heard more about the justice (or, as it was taught, the vengeance) of God, but I heard very little about the grace of God. God's grace should never be taught in isolation. We are expected to accept the sovereignty of God, believe on Him, and obey Him. Works of obedience are expected, for Jesus said "if you love me, you will keep my commandments." But there is a time when we have done all we could, and God's grace takes us the rest of the way. Be prepared; accept His grace; obey His precepts; love His indwelling presence.

What a tragedy it will be in the day of Judgment when God calls all people to stand before Him to be judged, only to hear Him say, "Depart from me!" There is a message from beyond the grave. It is spoken through the lips of the rich man in the Parable of the Rich Man and Lazarus. That message is: "Don't come here!" This great story that Jesus told is a warning to all of us who do not take "last things" as seriously as we ought. There will be a day of reckoning, or judgment. Someone has said that Jesus came the first time to be our Savior; the second time He comes will be to be Judge. He will sit on the throne of judgment (Matt. 25:31–46). Each of us will be accountable. My prayer for you is that you will remember the teachings of Jesus on the final things, the last things. Don't let the door be shut to you. Jesus spoke through the apostle John and said, "I stand at the door and knock." Open the door and let the Savior in. He will bring rich reward to all who will obey Him.

BIBLIOGRAPHY

Allen, C. Leonard. *The Cruciform Church: Becoming a Cross-shaped People in a Secular World*. Abilene, TX: ACU Press, 1990.

Arndt, William F. and F. William Gingrich. *A Greek-English Lexicon of the New Testament and Other Christian Literature*. Chicago: University of Chicago Press, 1979.

Barclay, William. *And Jesus Said: A Handbook on the Parables of Jesus*. Philadelphia: Westminster, 1970.

_____. *The Gospel of Matthew: The Daily Study Bible Series*. Philadelphia: Westminster, 1975.

_____. *The Gospel of Luke: The Daily Study Bible Series*. Philadelphia: Westminster, 1975.

Boice, James Montgomery. *The Parables of Jesus*. Chicago: Moody, 1983.

Bruce, Alexander Balmain. *The Parabolic Teaching of Jesus*. New York: A.C. Armstrong and Son, 1908.

_____. *The Synoptic Gospels*, in *The Expositor's Greek Testament*, edited by W. Robertson Nicoll. London: Hodder & Stoughton, 1912, Volume I.

Buttrick, George A. *The Parables of Jesus*. Grand Rapids: Baker, 1928.

Dodd, C.H. *The Parables of the Kingdom*. New York: Scribner's, 1961.

"Dropsy" in *The International Standard Bible Encyclopedia*, ed., James Orr. Grand Rapids: Eerdmans, 1955.

Hunter, Archibald M. *The Parables Then and Now*. Philadelphia: Westminster, 1971.

Jeremias, Joachim. *The Parables of Jesus*, 2nd ed. New York: Scribner's, 1972.

Kistemaker, Simon. *The Parables of Jesus*. Grand Rapids: Baker, 1980.

Lemley, Steven S. and Emily Y. Lemley. "The Elder Brother Was Right (And You Know It!). *Power for Today*, edited by Steven S. and Emily Y. Lemley, XXXIX, 1, 1994.

Lightfoot, Neil R. *Lessons from the Parables*. Grand Rapids: Baker, 1965.

Marshall, I. Howard. *Commentary on Luke: New International Greek Testament.* Grand Rapids: Eerdmans, 1978.

Matthews, Victor. *Manners and Customs in the Bible.* Peabody, MA: Hendrickson, 1988.

Meador, Prentice A., Jr. *Who Rules Your Life? Exploring the Kingdom Parables of Jesus.* Austin, TX: Journey Books, 1979.

Orr, James, editor. *The International Standard Bible Encyclopedia.* Grand Rapids: Eerdmans, 1955. Several articles from this source are quoted.

Plumptre, Edward Hayes. "Parable," in *Dr. William Smith's Dictionary of the Bible*, Volume III, ed., H.B. Hackett. Boston: Houghton, Mifflin and Co., 1870.

Robertson, A.T. *Word Pictures in the New Testament*, Volume I. Nashville: Broadman, 1930.

Sweet, Louis Matthews. "Tax" in *The International Standard Bible Encyclopedia*, ed., James Orr. Grand Rapids: Eerdmans, 1955.

Taylor, William M. *The Parables of our Saviour.* Grand Rapids: Kregel, 1975.

Trench, Richard Chevenix. *Notes on the Parables of Our Lord*, Popular Edition. Grand Rapids: Baker, 1948.

Wenham, David. *The Parables of Jesus.* London: Hodder & Stoughton, 1989.